The Curious Incident of the WMD in Iraq

D0802623

'It's clever, it's funny and it really makes you think' – Tony Hawks, comedian

'I've enjoyed reading it and it hits the nail on the head where Tony Blair is concerned' Charles Kennedy, MP

'A splendid stocking filler for all those who opposed the war, together with those who supported it but now feel they were mislead – which, as the author cheekily says, "covers just about everyone"' – Anthony Howard, *Times*

'A delicious book' – Nicholas Kent, Tricycle Theatre

'Alas it is a sad, sad story' – Tony Benn, MP

'Sharp and sly' – *Evening Standard*

'Great fun, and with a serious message' – David Seymour, Political Editor, *Daily Mirror*

'Curiously well researched' – *Sunday Herald*

Rohan Candappa lives in North London with his wife and children. He worked in advertising for 15 years. His favourite headline was for slug pellets that read 'Slugs slugs'. But it was never used. So now he writes books. He can often be found in the bookshops of North London sneakily moving his books to more prominent positions. It must work because he's sold over one million books. Mind you, he has got quite a large family.

Other Books by Rohan Candappa

The Curious Incident of the WMD in Iraq

By rohan candappa

PROFILE BOOKS

First published in Great Britain in 2004 by
Profile Books Ltd
58A Hatton Garden
London EC1N 8LX
www.profilebooks.co.uk

10 9 8 7 6 5 4 3

Typeset in Helvetica by MacGuru Ltd
info@macguru.org.uk

Printed and bound in Great Britain by
Bookmarque, Croydon, Surrey

A CIP catalogue record for this book is available from the British
Library.

ISBN 1 86197 900 2

Acknowledgements

Writing this book became a bit of an obsession for a while. I was convinced that I had to do it. And I was convinced I was the only one who could. And I was convinced that the world would be a better place once I had. So that's why I reckon I know what it's like to be Tony Blair. But I couldn't have written it without the support and encouragement of many people. First, and most important of all, there's Jan. Thank you. Then came Simon Trewin, Hannah McDonald, Andrew Franklin, Stephen Brough and Kate Griffin, and everyone at Profile Books. I'd also like to thank Trevor Horwood for his invaluable input and Daniel Mogford for his very fine cover design. And, of course, I would never have written this book if I hadn't been inspired by Mark Haddon's wonderful book *The Curious Incident of The Dog In The Night-Time*. A book which, if you haven't read yet, you really should.

I'd like to dedicate this book to everyone who opposed the war. And I'd also like to dedicate it to everyone who supported the war, but now feels that they were misled.

Which, when you think about it, covers just about everyone.

Rohan Candappa, October 2004

Important Caveat*

The intelligence this book is based on often comes from single, and possibly unreliable, and uncorroborated sources.

Indeed some of the intelligence may well turn out to be seriously flawed.

And in places more weight was placed on the intelligence than it could bear.

But it is clear that the author acted in Good Faith.

Which, of course, makes everything all right.

---

*N.B. This page is removable.

The Curious Incident of the WMD in Iraq

This Is The Introduction To This Book

I thought it was time to write a book to explain all about me. But I didn't have any ideas of my own. So I Thought About It and realised that the best place to get ideas about a book would be from another book. So I went to a very big bookshop where they also sell lots of different types of coffee including Mochaccinos which I like and asked the shop assistant a question.

This is the question I asked the shop assistant.

'What is your best book?'

And she said, 'What kind of book?'

And this wasn't any help so I asked her again. 'What is your best book?'

And she said, 'It all depends. Do you want a novel? Do you want a biography? Do you want a history book? Do you want a colouring book?'

And I said, 'What is your best book?'

And she did a look. The look she did was called Exasperated. And then she said, 'Our best book is *The Curious Incident Of The Dog In The Night-Time* by Mark Haddon.'

So I bought *The Curious Incident Of The Dog In The Night Time* by Mark Haddon and took it home and read it. And it is brilliant.

It is about a boy who is different from everybody else. And who Lives In A World Of His Own. And who Sees The World From An Odd Angle. And who Talks In A Funny Way. And who Always Tells The Truth.

And after I read the book I thought that I would write a book like this. But I didn't just copy Mark Haddon's book because after writing my book for a while I began to Develop Ideas Of My Own.

And then I thought what if people bought the book thinking it would be like Mark Haddon's book and later found out that it wasn't? And then I thought it doesn't matter because most people won't notice. Or if they do notice it will be too late because they will have already bought the book.

And it will be a lesson to them to Never Judge A Book By Its Cover.

This Is How This Book Starts

My name is Anthony Algernon St Michael Blair and I live at Number Eleven Downing Street. I know all the countries of the world and their capital cities and their Prime Ministers and the lyrics to every song recorded by The Rolling Stones who are The Greatest Rock'N'Roll Band In The World.

Lyrics are what the words in a song are called.

Oh yes, and I am Prime Minister. Being Prime Minister is the most important job in the country. The country that I am Prime Minister of is called the United Kingdom of Britain.

Ten years ago when I first met Alastair on Thursday The Twelfth Of May 1994 he showed me this picture:

And I knew that it meant 'In Opposition'.

Then he showed me this picture:

And I knew that it meant 'In Power', like when you're running the country and deciding about the economy, or asylum seekers, or building great big domes, or when you're still awake at three or four in the morning and you can walk up and down the Cabinet Office and pretend that you're the only person in charge.

Then Alastair drew some other pictures:

But I was unable to say what these meant.

I got Alastair to draw lots of these faces and then write down next to them exactly what they meant. I kept the piece of paper in my pocket and took it out when I didn't understand what someone was asking. But it was very difficult to decide which of the diagrams was most like the face they were making because people's faces move very quickly.

When I told Alastair that I was doing this, he got a pencil out and another piece of paper and said it probably made people very:

And then he laughed.

So I tore up the original piece of paper and threw it away. And Alastair apologised. And now if I don't know what someone is asking I answer a different question. Or I walk away.

What Alastair Thought
About This Opening

I showed Alastair this opening and asked what he thought.

Alastair said it was good and that I should write about something I would want to read myself. And I thought about this. And I realised that this was Good Advice. Alastair is always full of Good Advice. That's why I like him. That and his Blackburn Rovers boxer shorts.

The Book I Would Most Want To Read Myself

The book I would most want to read myself would be about Me. And about my Place In History. When I told this to Alastair he smiled. And then he said that the book would need An Angle. Something that would catch the readers' imagination. Something that would make it a mystery that had to be solved. Something that would be compelling. Something that would 'Sex It Up'.

So I said what about WMD?

And Alastair smiled again. But this time it was a slightly different smile.

So I am writing a Mystery Novel. About WMD. And about me.

And Alastair said, 'So it's two mysteries then.'

And then he laughed. But I didn't know what he meant.

How The Book Starts
After I 'Sexed It Up'

It was well after midnight. The WMD was lying in the sand in Iraq. It looked dangerous. It looked like it was ready to be used at very short notice. But the WMD was not ready to be used at very short notice. And it wasn't a WMD. It was just an ordinary missile. It was the kind of missile that you could find in any country in the world.

So why did we have to do a War?

Where It All Began

I asked Alastair what I should write next. And he said, 'Just tell the true story of the WMD. Start at the beginning. Go to the end. Then stop.'

And I thought that this was another of Alastair's Good Ideas. Because if I start at the very beginning where The Curious Incident Of The WMD In Iraq began then everyone would be able to understand everything about the WMD. And about me. And why I Had No Choice but to do a war with Mr Hussein.

So this is where The Curious Incident Of The WMD In Iraq began.

I was born at 6.10 a.m. on the Sixth of May in 1953 in Queen Mary Maternity Home in Edinburgh. And this is one of the Surprising Facets of me that many people don't know.

I am Scottish.

People don't know that I am Scottish because I don't speak with a Scottish brogue (which is a sturdy type of shoe). And I don't wear a kilt (which is a kind of skirt). And I don't get tanked up on 'heavy' and start fights for no reason (which is a popular Scottish hobby).

It is good to have Surprising Facets because it means that there is More To You Than Meets The Eye. This makes you Intriguing and Fascinating.

There is More To Me Than Meets The Eye. And I am Intriguing and Fascinating. And that is why Cherry who is my wife married me.

To help you understand all this I will draw some pictures.

This is a banana:

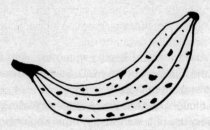

This is the same banana but now its skin has been unpeeled:

And inside the banana skin isn't a banana but there are two grapes, a lychee and a kumquat. This means that there is More To That Banana Than Meets The Eye. And that when you opened it what you discovered was Intriguing and Fascinating.

And it also means that you will never look at an unpeeled banana in the same way ever again because It Might Not Be What It Seems.

When I showed this to Alastair he said, 'That would be a good title for a book about you.'

And I said, 'What?'

And he said, 'Two grapes, a lychee and a kumquat.'

And I said, 'No, that would not be a good title.'

And he said, 'I was only joking.'

And I said, 'A book about a Prime Minister who does a War and makes the world a safer place with more people free from the rule of tyranny and also comes up with revolutionary and successful domestic initiatives like getting the police to march drunken yobbos to the nearest cash point machine so that they can pay On The Spot Fines and so realise that there are consequences to their bad behaviour and subsequently Mend Their Ways and become Responsible and Upstanding Members of the Community is not the kind of book that you should joke about.'

And he said, 'Sorry Tony.'

That's another thing about being Prime Minister. Sometimes the people who work for you Get Out Of Line. And then, because you are Prime Minister, you have to Exert Your Authority and Get Them Back In Line.

Or you can sack them. But I don't like sacking people. Sacking people isn't what I got into politics to do. It's much better if you get someone to Explain The Situation to them. In some detail. And then they Offer Their Resignation.

G'Day, Cobber

Another Surprising Facet about me is that when I was only one year old I went to live in Australia. This was long before *Neighbours*, or Kylie, or the Sydney Olympics so not many people had really heard about Australia.

I went with my family because my father had got a job in Adelaide.

When I was four years old there was a concert at school and I danced and sang a song as 'Mr Nobody'. I was a big hit. I liked it a lot. My mother found it very difficult to get me off the stage.

Because I spent some of my Formative Years in Australia I have always felt a Strong Affinity with the Australian people. This was to prove useful later on in life when I had to convince Mr Howard who is the Prime Minister of Australia to join with George and me in doing a War with Mr Hussein. I think my cheery greeting of 'G'day, cobber' always put Mr Howard at ease.

I also remembered from my time in Australia that Australians like things to be explained to them simply. And they like things to be explained to them over and over again. And they also like to think that they are at the centre of everything when in reality they really are a long way from everyone else and don't need to get involved at all.

But Mr Howard was very keen to join in. After I explained to George who Mr Howard was and where Australia was he was really happy to let him join in. I think what impressed George most was when I told him Australia had surfing just like in America.

I came back from Australia when I was four.

Skippy is from Australia. He is a bush kangaroo. He is very clever. He can communicate complex messages by making strange clicking noises that ordinary people can't understand.

Alastair used to call Robin 'Skippy'.

I am telling you all these things because they are something called Background. Background is very important if you want to understand What Is Really Going On. But when you are Prime Minister you are so busy that you don't always have time to know all the Background to the decisions that you have to take. This is just one of the Harsh Realities Of The Job.

That's why as Prime Minister I have people to read all the Background and Interpret It and tell me what is Important. And if sometimes they don't tell you the right things or leave things out that subsequently turn out to be Important that is Not Your Fault.

My Dad

My dad used to be Communist. This was when he was young. Then after the war he was Labour. Then after being an officer in the army for a few years and mixing with other officers he decided that he was really Conservative.

This is called a Change Of Heart.

People, like dads, can have a Change Of Heart. Politicians shouldn't have a Change Of Heart. It confuses the public. And it is a Hostage To Fortune that your political enemies will use against you whenever they can. And especially at Elections.

I have never had a Change Of Heart. And I have No Reverse Gear. This is something that The People respect. And it is one of the reasons that they chose me to Run The Country.

Alastair read this and said, 'A car that has no reverse gear isn't any good if it takes a wrong turn and drives into a dead end.'

But he didn't explain why that had anything to do with me.

My dad's great ambition was to become a Conservative MP. And after being a Conservative MP he wanted to go on to become a Conservative Prime Minister. But he had a stroke. So he couldn't.

The Futon Theory

If I was a psychologist I would probably mention The Futon Theory now. The Futon Theory is a theory that theorises that the loss of a father, or a father's failure, can be what spurs a son to get out from under the duvet on his Japanese bed (that converts into a sofa) and Succeed In His Father's Place.

But if The Futon Theory were true then I would have become a Conservative MP. And then a Conservative Prime Minister. But I became a Labour MP. And a New Labour Prime Minister. Which is completely different.

Psychologists always like looking for theories to explain things. They especially like looking for Significant Incidents In Childhood That Explain Things Later On.

If I was a psychologist which I am not because I am Prime Minister I might look at my childhood and say that:

the virtual loss of his father at such a significant stage in his development may well have led to his continual searching in his later life for a father figure or a succession of father figures to instruct him how to cope with and conquer the world, all of whom get dispensed with in time because none can ever match up to the actual and idealised father that was lost.

But I am not a psychologist so I probably won't say this.

When I discussed this theory with Aussie Pete, Peter M, Derry, Gordon and Alastair they all said it was rubbish. Except Alastair didn't say 'rubbish'. He said it was 'bollocks'.

Alastair is from The North.

School

When I was a small boy I went to Western Hill pre-prep school. My best subjects were English, Latin, Scripture and Games.

Games taught me a lot of Valuable Lessons For Life. I remember one race where I was tracking the boy in front all the way round. I waited for the final bend before Making My Move. And I knew I could beat him. But my legs just weren't strong enough.

I still won a silver cup. But it was not as big as the silver cup that the other boy won. And the Valuable Lesson that I learned from this Childhood Incident is that sometimes you need more than just Timing to win the race.

My cup   *His cup*

I also learned that I much prefer the big silver cup to the small one.

My favourite books were *The Lion, The Witch And*

The Wardrobe, *The Lord Of The Rings* and *Biggles Flies Undone*.

Big School

My Big School was Fettes College. My dad sent me there because it was the 'Eton Of Scotland'. Its most famous other pupil is James Bond. But James Bond was not a real pupil. That is because James Bond is a Made-Up Character. Whereas I am real and am a Not-Made-Up Character.

But in other ways I am Very Much Like James Bond. That is because he also saves the world from evil men hell bent on World Domination.

I won an Exhibition to go to Fettes College. An Exhibition is something that clever people win and means that your mum and dad pay less fees for you to go to school because you are so clever.

I was a Boarder at Fettes College. This means that you don't go home to see your mum and dad at the end of each day but have to stay at school and sleep in a big bedroom with lots of other boys. Just like Harry Potter. Except back then I couldn't do magic.

I Was Very Good At Making Toast

I hated Fettes College. It was beastly. I had to fag for one of the prefects.

Fagging is nothing to do with cigarettes or being homosexual. These ideas are what is called A Popular Misconception. And one of the reasons I am writing this book is to Dispel The Many Popular Misconceptions That Have Arisen.

Especially about me.

Fagging is to do with oppression.

I was oppressed by The System. And by the prefect. I had

to clean his shoes. I had to Blanco his army-cadet belt. I had to polish his buckle. I had to lay out his cricket whites. And I had to make his toast. It had to be no thicker or thinner than one inch which would be twenty-five millimetres today.

Some days I was even caned by the prefects.

This is why I am so affected by the suffering of the oppressed masses in the Third World. It is because I too have walked down that path.

You Never Forget A Good Teacher

My favourite teacher was Mr Anderson. Later on he became the headmaster of Eton. Eton is the Eton of England. After I became Prime Minister I appointed Mr Anderson Chairman of the Heritage Lottery and National Heritage Memorial funds.

When I was at school I used to call him 'sir'. Now that I am Prime Minister he is a 'Sir'. This is what is called One Of Life's Little Ironies.

'The Times They Are A Changin''

I was at school in the 1960s. At the time I thought this was a Creative and Vibrant time with Exciting Things Happening everywhere. Now I realise that the 1960s are to blame for so many of the Ills Of Today. And the 1960s are especially to blame for the rise in crime.

This is because the 1960s were an evil and pernicious time that planted the seeds of disaffection, disrespect and the breakdown of order that we see in The Youth Of Today. This is true even though The Youth Of Today were born in the late 1980s and early 1990s and shows just how evil the 1960s were.

But even a school as traditional as Fettes College couldn't resist the changes of the 1960s. This is why Mr Anderson set up a new house at the school. It was called

Ariston. It was to have no beating. And no fagging. It sounded Too Good To Be True.

I went on and on and on to Mr Anderson about joining Ariston. In the end he gave in. After I joined Ariston it became a big success. It was an example of how even the most rigid and tradition-bound institutions can be altered to keep up with the changing times. This proved to be a Valuable Lesson later on.

I was a big hit in Ariston house. I was good at cricket, rugger and Mick Jagger impressions. Mick Jagger is now called Sir Mick Jagger. That was another one of my Good Ideas.

'Friends, Romans, Countrymen ...'

One of my best skills at Fettes College was doing acting. Acting is pretending to be someone you're not.

The person I most liked acting was Mark Antony. He was in a play written by William Shakespeare. William Shakespeare was a Northerner from The Midlands and is sometimes called The Bard Of Avon which is a river in Bristol. He lived in a globe in Stratford which is in the East End Of London.

Mark Antony was in a play called Julius Caesar. He was a Roman. He was best friends with Caesar who was a soldier who became Emperor. But then Caesar got killed by people who were supposed to be his friends.

This is very clever of Shakespeare because it shows that even when you are in charge of everything you have to be On Your Guard. And you can't trust anyone. And you can't trust your friends either.

I can't remember much else because I was in the play such a long time ago. So I asked my friend Estelle who was my Education Secretary to buy the book *Julius Caesar York Notes For GCSE*.

York Notes For GCSE are good because they explain complicated things in simple ways so that you can pass exams. Explaining complicated things in simple ways is one of my Best Skills. It is very useful when you want to get elected for the first time. But when you want to be elected for the third time what is very useful is to explain simple things in complicated ways.

This is what *York Notes For GCSE* say about Mark Antony:

> *Until the death of Caesar, Antony is little more than a follower. His character becomes really defined when he gives a stirring ovation over Caesar's body, and shows a new side of himself. He is a skilful orator and easily turns the crowd to his way of thinking. Antony uses deliberate exaggeration or hyperbole in his speech in Act III Scene 2 in order to inflame the citizens of Rome. He shows that he is ruthless when in pursuit of the enemy. Antony is driven by his emotions and will not allow anything or anyone stand in the way of what he feels to be right.*

But I don't remember any of this.

I just liked it because I got to do an Oration. An Oration is a speech you do when someone is dead. I am good at Orations. And I liked it because Antony is my name. And I liked it because I got to say, 'Cry "Havoc" and let slip the dogs of war.'

I asked Alastair what kind of dogs the dogs of war were.

And he said 'Bulldogs. But not poodles. Or fucking Alsatians.'

'All Right, Broughton, I'm Coming'

My other best play was *Journey's End* by R. C. Sherriff.

It is a very good play but the title is confusing because it is not a play about the end of a journey at all but about a heroic and tragic captain called Captain Stanhope who is in charge of a group of soldiers in the trenches of the First World War.

The most notable person to play Captain Stanhope was Laurence Olivier when the play was first performed. I was the next most notable person to play Captain Stanhope and I was only a schoolboy.

Captain Stanhope is a hero because he is very brave and all his men love him. He is tragic because he is Weighed Down By The Heavy Burden Of Command. I too have been Weighed Down By The Heavy Burden Of Command. It is not a nice Heavy Burden to be Weighed Down By.

He and his men wait for the Brioche to make a Big Attack. The Brioche is another name for the Germans who were the enemy.* What everyone is really scared of is that the Brioche might attack using Phosgene which is a poison gas and so is a Chemical Weapon which is a WMD and is a Horrible Way To Die.

The play is Very Sobering and Makes You Think.

But there is a light-hearted moment in the play with a silly mistake that anyone could have made which involved a May Tree in bloom.

A May Tree In Bloom

---

*This is what is called a coincidence.

But mostly the play is serious.

This is because Stanhope is trapped by old-fashioned ideas of honour. And old-fashioned ideas of duty. And by circumstances he can't control. So he Has No Choice but to send out his men to do fighting of very little point because The Top Brass says so. Many of them will get killed which makes him sad.

You can tell that these Heavy Burdens Of Command are weighing Captain Stanhope down because he Obliterates Reality With Alcohol.

Luckily when the Heavy Burdens Of Command were weighing me down I didn't have to Obliterate Reality With Alcohol. I had My Faith instead.

The play had a real effect on me. That's why just before me and George went to do War against Mr Hussein I said:

That play had a real effect on me ... You have to isolate yourself when people are dying from what you yourself have chosen to do.

I also like the play because it meant that I could smoke on stage in front of the teachers and there was nothing they could do about it because it wasn't really me who was smoking it was Captain Stanhope. And you can't get into trouble for things that you do when you are only doing acting.

Rebel, Rebel

Another thing that I was good at at Fettes was opposing the Forces Of Conservatism. That's why I led and triumphed in the struggle to scrap Clause Three of the school rules that said the middle button of all school jackets had to be done up at all times.

Scrapping Clause Three was no more than a gesture. But it was important because it was a potent symbol of the Changing Times. And of my intent to change them.

I said to Mr Anderson, 'If I was running things I would go one better than scrapping Clause Three.'*

I also had very long hair which was Against The School Rules. I had very long hair because just like Mick Jagger I was a rebel who would never, ever conform to the Pre-scriptive And Oppressive Rules of The Establishment.

Then I got two As and a C at A-Level and went on to do reading Law at St John's College, Oxford.

---

*This is what is called a Prophetic Statement.

What I Did During My Gap Year

The first really interesting thing to note about my Gap Year is that I had one at all. This was long before Gap Years had been invented. This is just another example of how I was Ahead Of My Time. And it shows why I am so good at relating to The Young People Of Today.

Back then a Gap Year was something only public school kids who were going to Oxford or Cambridge did. And it is one of my top achievements as Prime Minister that now ordinary, poorer, less clever kids from Bog Standard Schools can do Gap Years as well.

In 1971 some kids would spend their Gap Year doing VSO which is Voluntary Service Overseas in India or Africa. And some kids would spend their Gap Year smoking marijuana and wearing Afghan coats in Marrakesh or Kathmandu.

For my Gap Year I chose a Tougher and altogether Less Well Travelled Path that led to me Roughing It in the decaying urban nightmare that was the cultural wasteland of a deprived part of inner city London teeming with coloured immigrants, a dispossessed white under-class, and all manner of social and societal ills.

Kensington was a revelation.

I stayed in a house belonging to a boy who had just left St. Paul's School. There were no grown-ups in the house and no house masters so we could stay up as late as we liked and play our music as loud as we wanted. So we did.

My favourite groups were Led Zeppelin, Cream and The New Seekers.

These were my favourite Led Zeppelin songs:

1 Stairway To Heaven
2 Black Dog
3 Rock'N'Roll

These are my favourite Cream songs:

1 Badge
2 White Room
3 Layla

This was my favourite New Seekers song:

1 I'd Like To Teach The World To Sing

'I'd Like To Teach The World To Sing' is a song about an Australian lady who would like to teach the world to sing. But she would like to teach the world to sing in Perfect Harmony.

That song had a big effect on me at the time. And it came back to me when I was trying to get everyone on the Security Council of the UN to vote for a Second Resolution so that me and George could do a War with Mr Hussein and invade Iraq and find and destroy his WMD and free the Oppressed Citizens Of That Benighted Country so they could get democracy. But no one would sing it with me, even though I'd got my friend Jack to photocopy the lyrics at the newsagents.

Vladimir and Gerhardt and Jacques said that my cover version was rubbish. Only my friend George joined in. After he turned the lyrics the right way up he really got into it. But when no one else would join in he got fed up. So he started to change the tune. And the words. And the beat got much faster than I could clap along to. In the end it was a completely different song. But I joined in anyway so that he wouldn't have to sing on his own. He's a rubbish singer when it's just him. And anyway it had more or less been my idea all along.

My Best Friend Clarence
In Kensington my best friend and constant companion was Clarence. Clarence was a purple guitar that I had made myself at home.

I used to practise the Riffs from my favourite songs on Clarence. A Riff is the memorable bit of a song that sticks in your mind that makes you want to go out and buy that song and so make the group who sing the song a big hit and the lead guitarist a Superstar and Love God.

This is a famous Riff:

Der, der, der
Der, der, de-der
Der, der, der
D-der

It is 'Smoke On The Water' by Deep Purple.
In many ways a Riff is a musical Soundbite.

Why I Am In Touch With Business
One of the reasons that in my political career I get on so well with business is that I too have been a businessman. And I have been a small businessman which is the hardest type of businessman of all to be. That's why I know about the constant struggle, the long hours, the petty bureaucracies, the foot-dragging inflexibility of an already overpaid workforce and the endless stress and frustration of having risked all to pursue a dream that you put your heart and soul and all the money you raised by remortgaging your house into.

I learned all this in my 11 months as a Rock Music Promoter.

The group I discovered, nurtured and managed were called JaDeD.

This was the slogan I came up with for JaDeD:

AVAILABLE FOR ALL DANCES, CONCERTS AND PARTIES
EXCITING ROCK-N-ROLL BAND

But I knew that if I really wanted to succeed I had to offer them something more, something new, something compelling. So I added:

SPACEMATIC DISCO WITH LIGHTS!

I think it was the exclamation mark that really set the pulses racing.

Then I opened an underground club called The Vineyard. It was very much like the famous Cavern Club in a back street of run-down Liverpool where The Beatles started. Except it was in Richmond. In a Congregational-ist church.

And because even then long before I had met Peter M I knew that presentation was important I made sure I had the right gear. Gear is what people used to call clothes back in those days.

This is a list of my best Gear:

1 Purple loons
2 Cuban heeled cowboy boots
3 Tight white flares with a lace-up fly

I also had hair that was even longer than the hair I had at school. This was because I was still a Rebel. I was a

Rebel and a Businessman. This is called a Conundrum. It too makes you Intriguing and Fascinating.

To get people to Hang Out at The Vineyard I would bicycle around all the girls' schools in Richmond and wait for the chicks to come out and I would tell them about JaDeD and the Happening Place with The Renegade Vibe that was The Vineyard.

My best line was to put my hands on my hips and say 'Let's Go Honeys'.

Lots of chicks would come to The Vineyard and would always want to talk to me. A friend who worked for me used to call them 'Blair's Babes'. This is a silly name which I Disapproved Of as it demeaned the chicks. And now I am much more Sophisticated because I don't call girls chicks any more. I call them Women and they are My Equal and I treat them with Respect. That's why when I became Prime Minister I let Women like Clare and Estelle be in charge of important things like International Development and Education.

Why I Understand All About Capitalism

On 16 February 1972 I paid JaDeD £30. And my management fee was 80 per cent of anything over £30. On 26 February 1972 I paid JaDeD £15. And my management fee was 100 per cent of anything over £15.

This was because I was adjusting the remuneration package of the workforce in accordance with changing fiscal conditions and productivity levels. And since I was the one taking all the risks surely it was only fair that I should reap the rewards.

And this shows how I am very good at Economics and Gordon should really let me have a go at Running The Economy Of The Country which I am sure I could do as well as being Prime Minister. But when I suggest this to Gordon all he does is talk about Prudence.

He talks about Prudence a lot. One day I suggested to Gordon that maybe I should meet her but he said we wouldn't get on though he didn't say why.

Alastair Gets Agitated

When Alastair read all this he started to get Agitated.

'What's wrong, Alastair?' I said.

He said, 'Tony, mate, all this bollocks about "what I did during the holidays" is a little bit interesting but what has any of it got to do with anything important?'

'It's Background, Alastair,' I said.

He said, 'It's bollocks. No one gives a toss about it, mate. It's just a load of old wank. I mean, what has any of it got to do with the War In Iraq?'

And I looked at him and gave him one of my most Enigmatic Looks that I had learned from watching Arsène Wenger on *Match Of The Day* and said:

'Alastair, The River That Was The War Was Fed By Many Tributaries.'

Which Stopped Him In His Tracks.

Then he said, 'That's a good line.'

And I said, 'I know.'

And he said, 'Whose is it?'

And I said, 'Sir Christopher Meyer.'

And he said, 'That poncey Ambassador we had in Washington during the War?'

And I said, 'Yes.'

And he said, 'That's a very good line.'

And then I gave him an Even Profounder Look and said:

'And in those tributaries many small fish and even water boatmen swim around or skate across the surface of the water looking for things to eat like little plants or teeny-tiny insects that you can only see with a microscope and that teem amongst the flotsam and jetsam and shopping trolleys and carrier bags that clog up the eddying currents of the fast flowing turgid and vivacious water.'

And he said, 'That's one of your lines, isn't it?'

And I said, 'Yes.'

And he said, 'Stick to the shorter line.'

And then he said, 'And I still think you should get to the stuff about the war quicker.'

And I said, 'But I want people to understand Who I Am and All I Have Achieved and My Place In History.'

And he said, 'Then you should get to the stuff about the war quicker.'

And this time he looked at me with one of his most profound looks.

'OK then,' I said.

And I did the next chapter of my story.

What I Did At Uni

I went to University and discovered God and Politics.

What Happened After I Showed This Chapter To Alastair

I showed this chapter to Alastair.

He said, 'It's a bit short.'

There's a Good Phrase I know that you can use when something like this happens. This is the Good Phrase: *There's no pleasing some people*.

So I used this phrase.

'There's no pleasing some people,' I said.

And Alastair said, 'Maybe you should explain about what you did at university a bit more.'

And I said, 'OK then.'

And he said, 'Except leave out God.'

And I said, 'I can't leave out God.'

And he said, 'Tony, mate, how many times do I have to tell you: we don't do God.'

So I thought about what Alastair had said and decided that for me to present myself to the public without telling them how important God is to me and how my Faith is the Background to every decision I take would be Very Misleading. And the last thing I want to do is Mislead The Public.

A Bit More About What I Did At Uni

At Uni I did reading Law. Law is a very hard subject and only really clever people do well at it. I did well at it. Although I would have done a lot better if I had studied harder.

But I was being A Typical Uni student and doing all the usual things that students did like rowing in an eight and belonging to a pseudo-archery club called the St. John's Archery Club whose main point was to hold parties and wear straw boaters and blazers and allow chicks only as guests on 'Ladies' Days'. It was very much like being in The Young Ones.*

I also stayed up late into the night, drinking coffee, and putting the world to rights with other Like Minded Chums. My best LMC was Aussie Pete who was a Renegade Priest from Australia. He taught me about how God was really a socialist. And how it is only through our interactions with society that we can be fully ourselves as individuals. And how religion is only truly valid if it actively and practically helps societies and individuals achieve their true potential.

So Aussie Pete was a rebel who would often attack the organisation, structure, actions and preoccupations of The Church as being hopelessly out of touch and irrelevant to the Changing World Of Today. I really looked up to him.

---

*That is 'The Young Ones' the Sir Cliff Richard song, not The Young Ones the television series.

I Discover A Philosophy

Aussie Pete got a lot of his ideas from a Scottish (like me) thinker of the 1930s called John Macmurray. What made John Macmurray special is that he put the idea of The Community at the centre of it all.

Much later on, when I wanted to become Leader of the Labour Party and I realised I needed a Philosophy, I remembered all this and decided that it had been My Philosophy all along.

Ugly Rumours

At Uni I also decided that whilst I had been a very successful Rock Music Promoter what I really wanted to do was to be the lead singer of a band.

The band that I became the lead singer of was called The Ugly Rumours. All the other band members came from Winchester School so I fitted right in. I think I made a very good impression at the audition because I turned up on time and had written down all the lyrics to my favourite songs.

My strengths as a lead singer were my Good Stage Presence, my Patter, my Sexy Hip Wriggling, and my Tight Trousers. My weaknesses were my singing.

And my refusal to sleep with groupies or smoke marijuana. Marijuana was a drug and was illegal. And it is wrong to do things that are illegal.

(Luckily when I got to be Prime Minister I discovered that I got to have an Attorney General who can tell you when things are legal or not legal. And the best thing is that when we decide that things are legal, then we *can* do them, and we don't have to tell anyone why!)

My best bits of Patter on stage were:

1 'Hello. We're The Ugly Rumours. Let's Rock!'

2 'Hey, Corpus Christi, 'Ow are yer?'

3 'We're Tough On Pop, And Tough On The Causes Of Pop.'

And then I would launch into the opening lines of 'Honky Tonk Woman'. The Ugly Rumours were a big success.

In all we played six jigs.

Then we split up due to Musical Differences. But I've never lost my love of Rock'N'Roll. And I've never got rid of Clarence.

And when I was elected Prime Minister and had a big bash at my new place I got Noel Gallagher of the rock group Gallagher and Lyle to stay behind after everyone had gone for a little after hours 'jam' session. He wasn't keen at first, but when I told him I was 'mad for it' he saw that we spoke the same language and stayed.

He was very impressed. He said he'd never heard 'Wonderwall' played that way before. I told him he could borrow my wah-wah pedal any time he wanted. But he must have bought his own because he's never been round since.

Norwegian Blues

The other thing I liked at Uni was watching a comedy programme on television called *Monty Python's Flying Circus*. It was very funny although there wasn't a python in it called Monty.

My favourite sketch on *Monty Python* (as we called it) was a sketch called The Dead Parrot Sketch in which a man goes into a pet shop from which he had bought a parrot and complains to the pet shop owner that the parrot had been dead all along and the pet shop owner just Denies What Is Obviously True over and over and over again. In the end the man with the dead parrot just gives up and leaves. It was a Very Funny Sketch.

My other favourite *Monty Python* sketch was a cartoon in which cartoon bombs are falling on a cartoon city and all the cartoon buildings are being reduced to cartoon rubble and a little cartoon van with a cartoon loudspeaker on top drives around saying:

'We apologise for any inconvenience.'

It was a Very Funny Sketch too.

I showed all this to Alastair and this is what he said: 'I'm pleased you dropped the stuff about God.'

And I said, 'I'm not going to drop it, Alastair. I just haven't put it in yet.'

And he could see that I had Made My Mind Up. And Alastair knows that when I have Made My Mind Up then That's That and Nothing Will Change My Point Of View.

And then he said, 'Tony, mate, when you bang on about God it's about as clear as a dodgy dossier.'

So I decided to 'humour him'. 'Humouring someone' is when you do something that you don't really want to, or need to, but you do it because you know it will make that person feel better and not ignored.

So I said, 'OK then, Alastair, I'll make it clearer.'

And he said, 'Good. So how are you going to do that?'

And I said, 'I'll draw some pictures.'

And then Alastair said, 'Well, that should fucking work.'

And then he left the room.

I love it when Alastair gets so enthusiastic about my ideas that he has to leave the room.

Some Drawings That Explain The Stuff About God And My Philosophy For Life Etc.

This is an individual

This is a group of individuals

As you can see when the individual is on his own he is Sad. But when he is in a group of individuals he is Happy.

And when he explains to all the other individuals that he is Happy because his relationships with the other individuals in the group do not confuse and confine him but define and liberate him they too become Happy.

And the name for this group of Happy individuals is a Community.

This is God

And this is where many people think God lives

And this is how many people think God relates to people

But this is wrong because if God is to be of any practical use to people he must Get Offa His Cloud and join with the people to make their lives better. Which is why:

God is a socialist

And if people need to achieve a common end God joins in too and so is relevant and responsive to the needs of The People.

God joining in too

So my God really is The People's God. And this is why my relationship with God is not a personal relationship, but more a social one. And it is a social one based on the idea of The Community.

But just because my God is a Socialist doesn't mean that he is a namby-pamby lefty who explains away vandalism and mugging old ladies and people throwing fast food boxes on the pavement even though there is a litter bin right next them as being the fault of 'society'.

No, my God is a hard core moralist who sees the world in Black & White. Like I do.

Which is why I believe in the Unfashionable Concepts of Good and Evil.

The best way to explain this is with this diagram:

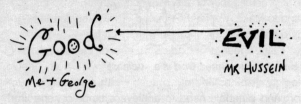

And because I Am My Brother's Keeper and Will Not Walk By On The Other Side and because I believe in Personal Responsibility, I Had No Choice but to do war with Mr Hussein and topple his evil regime.

So I did.

What My Relationship With God Is Really Like
But what is my relationship with God really like?

Well, to help you understand let me explain it to you in Rock'N'Roll terms.

God writes the Songs. Jesus was the Lead Singer. And I am just the Front Man for a Tribute Band.

A Fork In The Road*

When I was at Uni I thought about going into the church.†
But I decided that if I really wanted to Achieve Something
and to Make A Difference that I Had No Choice but to go
into politics.

I also thought that the structure of the church was
'too archaic, anachronistic, riddled with petty ideo-
logical disputes and out of touch with and irrelevant to
ordinary people' for me to have any chance of achieving
anything.

So I joined The Labour Party.

---

*This is what is known as a metaphor. There wasn't really a fork in
the road. Or a road.
†Which means *the* church not *a* church, because of course I have
gone into lots of churches.

Derry, Cherry, Charlie And Me

When you want to become a lawyer you become A Pupil again. But this is not like being a pupil at school. And anyway I Had Changed. So I didn't want to do any Rebelling Against Authority. This is because I had realised that the best way to rebel against authority was to Become The Authority and then you can Rebel From Within.

My teacher was called Derry. He was very clever. He had a brain the size of a melon. I have wondered about what kind of melon he had a brain the size of and I have decided that it was probably a honeydew melon.

When Alastair read this he said, 'And an ego the size of a watermelon.'

This is called Extending The Metaphor.

Then Derry became my boss and he taught me lots and lots. And he mainly taught me to do Analytical Thinking and to do Gravitas which is all about looking serious at Appropriate Moments.

Later on when I became Prime Minister I made Derry Lord Chancellor so I became his boss. This is called A Reversal Of Fortunes and is often used as a dramatic device in novels and films.

Later on we had A Disagreement About Wallpaper Amongst Other Things.

So I had to let him go.* But I gave his job of Lord

---

*This is what is called a Euphemism. A Euphemism is a way of saying something so that it sounds nicer than it really is. I like Euphemisms. Another example of a Euphemism is 'Friendly Fire'. Or 'I Accept Full Responsibility'.

Chancellor to Charlie who was a pal from before Uni and who had rented me a room in his house when I first became a lawyer.*

'There She Stood, In The Street ...'

The other person I met at this time who was An Important Influence On My Life was Cherry who is my wife. She was much cleverer than me. And she was much more keen on The Labour Party because she had grown up in a Poor Working Class area of Liverpool in The North.

We met when we were both applying for the same job. I got it and she didn't. Later on we both stood for Election as Labour MPs. I became one and she didn't. But she was good enough to have got the job. And good enough to have been an MP. But her Ambition was not as great as my Ambition. So she supported me in my drive to the top.

I fell in True Love with her. I had No Choice but to marry her. She eventually agreed.

Learning The Ropes

What happened next was that I Learned The Ropes. This is another metaphor and has nothing to do with ropes. It is an expression that means you learn the basics of How Things Work.

The main basic I learned of How Things Worked in The Labour Party was that they didn't work very well. That is because The Labour Party Was Too Old Fashioned.

While the Conservative Party could see that next year's trend would be Big Shoulder Pads and Power Dressing

---

*Charlie was also one of the people who had made The Millennium Dome such a big success and such a Potent Symbol of New Labour.

The Labour Party was still wearing Hob-Nailed Boots and Dungarees. While the Conservative Party supermodel was Mrs Thatcher, the Labour Party had Mr Callaghan and then Mr Foot.

Even I could see that if you Wear The Wrong Clothes To The Party It Is Very Unlikely That Anyone Will Ask You To Dance.

(I write this to show that Alastair's not the only one who can Extend A Metaphor.)

What The Labour Party Was Good At

But there was one thing that The Labour Party was Very Good At. The Labour Party was Very Good At Infighting. Infighting is when people who are on the same side fight with each other.

And just like a fight in a playground at school everyone else gathers round and shouts 'Fight! Fight! Fight!' and waits to see who will win. But when there's a fight at school a teacher always looks out of the window of the Staff Common Room after a while and sees what's going on and comes and breaks things up. But in The Labour Party there were no teachers to break up the fights. So the fights never ended.

And the only one who won was Mrs Thatcher.

The fights were always about how Left the party should be. And it wasn't simple because there were so many different types of Left. These are some of the different types of Left:

Soft Left
Centre Left
Left
Medium hard Left
Hard Left

Well hard Left
Loony Left
Ken
Derek

Everyone always wanted to know what type of Left you were. They wanted to know where you played in the team.

Later on as I started to get picked for the first team I realised that my best position was a fluid one. I was an overlapping wing back, playing on the left, but switching flanks if the opportunity arose to get in some good crosses from the right.

The problem was that we lacked a decent centre forward.

(I write this to show that Alastair's not the only person to know about football.)

The other thing I was good at was wearing badges. At the time it was very important to wear the right badges. My best badge was a CND badge. I used to wear it all the time. But I think it must have fallen off my jacket recently and got stuck down the back of the wardrobe because I haven't seen it for ages.

The Other Important Thing That Happened To Me During This Period

The Other Important Thing That Happened To Me During This Period is that I got elected to Parliament. And when I got elected to Parliament I was The Youngest Member Of Parliament In The House Of Commons. And this was A Quite Considerable Achievement.

But before you can get elected to Parliament you have to be selected for a constituency. The whole country is divided up into constituencies and every constituency gets to send the person they elect to sit in The House Of Commons where the Laws Of The Land are made.

This is called Democracy. And it is the best way to run things. In Iraq before Me and George did War with Mr Hussein they did not have Democracy. They had Dictatorship. And that is one of the reasons that we did War so that the People of Iraq could have Democracy and elect their own government.

How I Was Selected To Be A Labour Candidate

This is how I was selected to be the Labour candidate in Sedgefield which is in The North.

When I heard that the Labour Party in Sedgefield were looking for a candidate I drove up in my brown Mini Metro who I'd always secretly called Shadowfax and went to see the people who could select me or nominate me as we say.

They were a group of men, lounging about on sofas and armchairs watching the European Cup Winners' Cup Final between Aberdeen and Real Madrid. They were about to decide my future. And so the future of the country. And so the future of the world.

The game went to extra time. Luckily I knew lots about 'footie' so I could join in the conversations. Here is a list of some of the things I said:

1 Good shot!
2 He was never off side!
3 She fell over! She fell over!
4 Yeeeeeeees!
5 We shall not, we shall not be moved!
6 Go right! Go right!
7 It's coming home, it's coming home, football's coming home!*

Afterwards I told them that one of the reasons that I should be chosen was that I was against the power in the party residing in unrepresentative groups of men in smoke-filled rooms. When I said this they all stopped smoking and decided to choose me as their candidate.

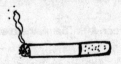

This is a cigarette like the cigarettes that made the smoke that filled the rooms where unrepresentative

---

*This is a song that I made up but later remembered and used really well when I had become Leader of The Labour Party and was making a stirring and memorable speech to The Labour Party conference just before we were about to go and fight the Election that we won for the first time in seventeen years.

*groups wielded the real power in The Party. This is
something I was against and shows why the accusations
that I amended government policy after Mr Ecclestone
gave £1,000,000 to The Party are obviously ludicrous as I
have always been against smoking.*

I Get Elected

After I got selected as a candidate the next thing I had to do
was get elected. So I did. Elsie Tanner who later became
my mother-in-law came and campaigned for me. This is
called a Celebrity Endorsement. Celebrity Endorsements
are good because if you stand next to the Celebrity while
they're doing the Endorsing then you stand a very good
chance of getting your picture in the papers.

Other things that Celebrities Endorse include Everest
Double Glazing, Stannah Stair Lifts and Benecol. I won
the election by 8,000 votes: 21,000 people voted for me,
13,000 people voted for the Conservative candidate and
10,000 people voted for the SDP candidate. This means
about 2,000 more people voted against me than for
me, but I was still the winner. This is How Democracy
Works.

But in that Election Mrs Thatcher did a bigger win than
me.

Why I Am Not Like Mrs Thatcher

One of the best things about this book is that it gives
me the opportunity to Put The Record Straight. That's
because even though I am The Prime Minister and am
in charge of everything to do with running the country it
is really surprising how often people get it wrong about
what kind of person I am.

For example lots of people who should be my friends
think that I am like Mrs Thatcher. In fact, when I first

became an MP I spent a lot of time attacking Mrs Thatcher about all the things she was doing that were wrong.

When I showed this bit to Alastair he said it 'lacked balls'. Balls is when you're tough about something. And tough on the causes of something. Alastair said that I should come up with a concrete example of how I attacked Mrs Thatcher to show how completely different I was from her.

So I have.

In *The New Statesman* magazine on the seventh of November 1986 I attacked Mrs Thatcher about The Westland Affair. This was a Secret Affair about the awarding of government contracts to build helicopters. When I delved into the murky waters of this Secret Affair I knew that this was a Time For Action.

These are some of the things that Mrs Thatcher had done that were wrong:

1 Had a letter written and allowed it to be leaked.
2 Blamed officials for the leak.
3 Denied ministerial responsibility for the actions of a department.
4 Undermined the whole concept of ministerial responsibility and hence undermined Parliament's ability to hold the ministers and their departments accountable for their actions.
5 Not punished any civil servant or minister for the whole mess in the hope that the public would soon get bored of it all and allow her to Get Away With It.

I Cogently and Coherently attacked all this in the article. And I also mentioned her fiddling of the unemployment figures, politicisation of the civil service and myriad attacks on the BBC.

I rounded off this Blistering Attack on Mrs Thatcher with this Heartfelt condemnation:

> *What really distinguishes the modern Tories from the old, or Thatcher from Heath, is that they want, above all, to win. It is an obsession. For her and for those like her, scruples simply clutter up the path to victory.*

So you can see I Am Completely Different From Mrs Thatcher.

The Wilderness Years

But the main thing that happened over all these years is that The Labour Party lost elections. We lost election after election after election. Losing elections was The Labour Party's very best skill.

And it was all because we were always doing Infighting.

I realised that Something Had To Be Done so I wrote a Hard-Hitting And Provocative paper that Tackled The Issue Head On. I circulated it to all the important people in The Labour Party. It was called 'In Place Of Strife'.

Because it has become such an Important Document in the history of The Labour Party I am reprinting it here in full. This is what it said:

In Place Of Strife
by
Anthony Algernon St Michael Blair

Would everyone please, please, please stop fighting!

It was heady stuff. But even this was not enough to Get People To See Sense. I was Sad that I hadn't managed to alter the course of the party with my Radical Solution. But I needn't have worried because my bold approach had been noticed by two people who were to help me change the history of politics in Britain. And the world.

They approached me in a side passage of the House Of Commons and the one with the moustache said: 'Hello, my name's Peter and this is my friend Gordon.'

And I said, 'Hello, Peter and Gordon.'*

And Peter said, 'I'm very clever, very good at scheming and very good at getting people to look their best and Gordon often has a chip on his shoulder but is steeped in The Labour Party right to his Very Soul and has a Brilliant Political Mind.'

And I said, 'Crikey!'

And Peter said, 'Let's all get together and Modernise The Labour Party.'

And I said, 'Great!'

So we did.

How We Modernised The Labour Party

We Modernised The Labour Party by sitting around late in the night and Putting The World To Rights. It was great. It was just like being back at Uni. Except this time we were Really Going To Make A Difference. And we called what we were doing The Project.

One of the ways Peter helped me look my best was by getting me to change my name. He said I should call myself Tony. He said that would give me The Common Touch. So I did.

It was very clever. Because I was still the same person. But just by changing my name it changed the way people Perceived me. Peter talked a lot about Perception. But a lot of it was quite complicated. So I just nodded my head a lot and said 'Yes' quite slowly. This is a Good Technique to use when you don't understand what's going on but still want to Look Intelligent.

---

*This was not the 1960s singing duo Peter and Gordon as I first thought but two other men entirely.

What I Understood About Perception

One day after he had been Going On About It For Quite Some Time Peter asked me what I understood about Perception. I hadn't really been listening so I just said the first thing that came into my head.

I said, 'It rhymes with Deception.'

Peter looked at me in a different way and then he said, 'You're smarter than you look, aren't you?'

The other thing that Peter was right about was Gordon. Gordon did have a Brilliant Political Mind. And he was already a High Flyer in the party. I looked at Peter and Gordon and thought, 'Gosh, if these chaps only let me Hang Out with them I could learn So Much.'

Brothers In Arms

One night when we sitting around sorting out the future of The Labour Party I told Peter and Gordon that this was just like being back at Uni. Peter asked me what posters I had on my bedroom walls and I said Mick Jagger. And Gordon said he had Che Guevara. And I said who was he and Gordon and Peter looked at each other and then looked back at me. Then they explained all about Che Guevara.

And when they explained about him I realised that Cherry had had a picture of him on her bedroom wall when I first met her, but that I had always thought that it was David Essex.

Then Peter suddenly got very excited. He said that when Che and his friend Fidel had started the revolution in Cuba they had landed on a beach with only a handful of Brothers In Arms. But this handful of brothers had eventually led The People in a triumphant revolution that freed the island from tyranny. And then he said that's who we're like. We're like a band of brothers from Cuba!

And I said, 'You mean like The Gibson Brothers?'

And Gordon said, 'No, what Peter meant was that we're revolutionaries and we need to organise ourselves and our actions along those lines.'

Then Peter said, 'We all have a role to play.'

So I said, 'What role can I play? Because I am very good at acting.'

And Peter said, 'You can be Che. And Gordon can be Fidel.'

And then I said, 'But who are you going to be?'

And Peter said, 'I'll be Lennon. He was the visionary. He was the idealist. He had the ideas.'

And the funny thing is I had never thought of Peter as a Beatles fan.

The Revolution (And This Time It Will Be Televised)

Peter and Gordon got really excited about this Revolution idea. And they went away and came up with a plan. They drew the plan on a chart. The chart had nine boxes. And when they explained it all to me I got A Little Confused.

So as I listened I nodded my head and every now and again said 'Yes' quite slowly. But then Peter asked me What I Thought About It All. And I didn't know what I thought about it all so I said the first thing that came into my head.

'A Revolution. That's something that goes round. Like a circle.'

Then I gave a Meaningful Look.

I didn't know what I was talking about. But luckily Peter did.

'That's brilliant. That's quite brilliant,' he said.

Then he went away and redrew his chart. And when he came back it wasn't a chart. And it didn't have any boxes on it. It was a circle. With arrows. And if you followed the arrows you could go round and round the circle for ever. And you would never have to get off.

And this was the chart. It was a plan of action. It was called The Unfinished Revolution because there would be no end to it. Ever.

The Unfinished Revolution

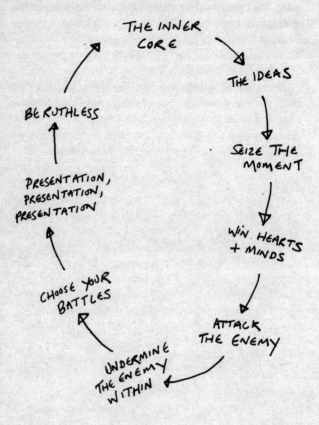

This is an explanation of The Unfinished Revolution.

The Inner Core

This was Peter and Gordon and me. We were the ones in charge. We were the ones who made the decisions.

But as well as the Inner Core there was also the outer core. This was Alastair who was a Tabloid Newspaper Man. And Philip who used to be an ad-man, Wore Glasses and was Good At Maths. And Anji who was a girl I'd met at school and who'd been keen on me ever since. Though Not In That Way.

There were no Black People in the outer core. Looking back this was a mistake. But now that I am Prime Minister I make a point of choosing Black People for important government posts. And not just because they're Black. But because they're Good Enough To Do The Job.*

---

*The top Black Person in the government today and who is actually in the Cabinet is Peter H from South Africa. He is a famous Black Person who single handedly caused the collapse of the racist system of apartheid in South Africa by stopping people playing rugger.

His catchphrase was that 'people should not be judged on the colour of their skin'. Which is good for him because he is actually orange.

These are My All Time Top Three Black People:

1 Martin Luther King
2 Muhammad Ali
3 Jimi Hendrix

Oh, and I've just thought of another one:

4 Nelson Mandela

The Ideas

One of the top jobs of the Inner Core was to come up with Ideas. One of our best ideas was:

The world has changed, so must the Labour Party

This was The Big Idea. We also thought that we had to reinvent Labour. We wanted it to be 'the credible expression of a new relationship between society and the individual'.

Underneath The Big Idea were The Medium Sized Ideas. And underneath The Medium Sized Ideas there were The Small Ideas. And underneath The Small Ideas were the Teeny-Tiny Ideas.

We often argued as to whether ideas were medium sized, or small or teeny-tiny. But we never argued about The Big Idea. We all agreed on that.

This is an example of an idea that we argued about.

And I think I'd probably have to rewrite the list because Nelson Mandela is such a Wise, Heroic and Inspirational figure. So here's the new list:

1 Nelson Mandela
2 Martin Luther King
3 Muhammad Ali
4 Jimi Hendrix

Unfortunately Mr Mandela is now quite old and doesn't really understand the true nature and complexity of global politics today which is probably why he was against Me and George doing War with Mr Hussein. But I don't hold this against him.

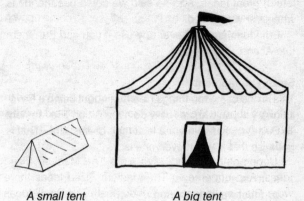

A small tent   *A big tent*

Some thought Labour should be A Small Tent with only people who agreed with you inside it. I thought it should be A Big Tent with lots of people inside who agreed with you about some things but not with others.

When I suggested this someone asked but what happens to the people in The Big Tent when they want to talk about the things they disagree with us on? And I said, 'Well, that's the secret of the Big Tent. We only ever talk about the things everyone agrees on.'

We had lots of ideas.

And when we ran out of ideas we went to America where McDonald's Happy Meals come from and got more ideas from Bill who was President and who became my Best Friend when I became Prime Minister.* He had

---

*A lot of people have asked how can George who is President now be My Best Friend, when Bill who used to be President used to be My Best Friend, and they are two such different people especially ideologically? And it's easy because friendship is not based on ideology. It's based on getting on with someone and

lots of great ideas. And he said we could use the ideas whenever we wanted.

But ideas are only ever any use if you can Put Them Into Action.

Seize The Moment

This is one of the top things I learned about being a Revolutionary. If you want to really do a revolution The Moment To Seize is when everyone is at their Lowest Ebb. That is because that is when everyone is:

a. least able to resist
b. most wanting change
c. most willing to be led.

For Peter, Gordon and Me that Moment should have been when The Labour Party Lost Its Fourth Election In A Row.

Everyone was Despondent. Everyone wanted A Change.

But the Moment came too soon for us. Peter, Gordon and Me just weren't ready. And Mr Smith became leader instead.

Mr Smith kind of wanted to change things, but not

---

having fun on holiday together with them and finding common interests like God or Colgate toothpaste and finding things you agree on and only talking about those things like doing war with Mr Hussein and not bringing up things you disagree on like global warming and The International Court Of Criminal Justice and whether football is called football or soccer. And anyway people are missing the most important thing that Bill and George had in common. Their job.

much. And he was still too much like the Old Labour Party. So we decided to Bide Our Time.

Biding Your Time is what you do if you have a Cunning Plan but can't do the Cunning Plan yet.

So we started to Argue Our Corner and State Our Case and in that way Win Hearts And Minds.

Winning Hearts And Minds

This is what you have to do if you want to Get The People On Your Side.

It's important to Get The People On Your Side if you want to do a Revolution because only The People can throw The Powers That Be out with any legitimacy. Then they give you the power and you can be in charge and tell them what to do.

If you don't Get The People On Your Side before you throw out The Powers That Be then what you are doing is not a Revolution but a Coup which is bad. A Coup is all about seizing power but a Revolution is about getting The People to seize power than hand it over to you.*

Some people in the Labour Party called Militant wanted to do a Coup. But they shouted too much to Win The Hearts And Minds Of The People. When we were trying to Win Hearts And Minds we didn't do any shouting. We did chatting.

We found that the best chatting to do to Win The Hearts And Minds Of The People was about *their* hopes

---

*There is of course another way which is A Liberation. That's when you do an invasion, overthrow the Powers That Be, install a regime of friends and declare that you're bringing Democracy to The People, but in fact you have to stay in charge behind the scenes or Anarchy May Result. So a Liberation is a Coup that you pretend is a Revolution.

and *their* fears. You always have to chat about fears first and then move on to hopes. That way your chatting will be Uplifting. Do it the other way and it will be Depressing.

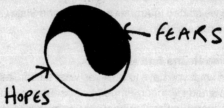

Attack The Enemy

The Enemy is the people who are against you. That's why you have to do attacks with them. I already knew about this.

(For example, Mr Hussein was an Enemy. That's why we had to do an attack with him and we also had to do an attack with him before he did an attack with us.

This is a brand-new doctrine in International Relations that George thought of called Pre-emptive Action that Clearly Makes The World A Much Safer Place. I didn't understand it at first but then Alastair explained it to me like this:

'It's like if I go to a Blackburn Rovers football match and as I'm walking to the game I see a Burnley fan walking towards me and I know that in the past Burnley fans have been violent bastards so rather than wait for him to attack me with the flick knife he might have in his jacket I twat the fucker with a sledgehammer while he's looking the other way. It's like equalising before the other side scores. To be honest, given all the circumstances, there's no other choice. And suppose I do nothing and he attacks me, or worse still, the defenceless little blind kiddie who's walking to the match next to me? And, obviously, it makes going to football matches a whole lot safer for everyone.'

Alastair's very good at explaining things. He's helped me understand loads of complicated things. Like the offside rule. But he's wrong about private schools.)

Undermine The Enemy Within

Peter has taught me lots of stuff that's been especially useful since I've been Prime Minister. Before I met him I never even knew that there were Enemies Within.

Enemies Within are people who are On Your Side, but not On Your Side enough. They are people who have Other Points Of View or A Different Interpretation Of The Facts.

Before I met Peter I thought that people with Other Points Of View or who had A Different Interpretation Of The Facts were good because they encouraged debate and helped make a Vibrant Democracy. But Peter explained that this isn't what happens.

What happens is that these people weaken your argument, confuse The People (whose Hearts And Minds you're trying to *Win*) and drain your energy. And anyway their Other Points Of View and Different Interpretations Of The Facts are always wrong. So it's far better not to let them do any of these things. Which is why you have No Choice but to undermine them.

This is sneaky and cunning but Totally Justified because of something called The Greater Good. The trick here is to make sure that it's always you who says what The Greater Good is.

Peter was top banana at all this, but he pretends he wasn't. His best wheeze was called 'Briefing Against Colleagues'. But I don't know how to do it because Peter always made sure I left the room while it was going on. That's how thoughtful he is.

And the really surprising thing about The Enemy Within who you have to Brief Against is that they often turn out to be people you really like, admire and respect like Mo or Robin or Clare or even my Close Personal Friend Gordon who I was surprised to read in a newspaper in 1998 had 'psychological flaws'!

But obviously all this was far off in the future.

Choose Your Battles Carefully
This bit is very simple. Don't fight battles that you can't win.

Presentation, Presentation, Presentation
This was Peter's top area.

He understood that today The People were so bombarded by Information that very little of it stuck. And that most of the time most of The People weren't interested in politics. So *how* you presented something was almost as important as *what* you presented.

And Peter had worked in Television. So he knew how Television worked. And he knew what worked on Television.

And Alastair had worked in the Tabloids. So he knew how the Tabloids worked. And he knew what worked in the Tabloids.

And Philip With The Glasses had worked in Advertising. So he knew how Advertising worked. And he knew what worked in Advertising.

And by this point in the never-ending cycle of The Unfinished Revolution I had learned quite a lot of Useful Stuff from Peter and Gordon and Alastair and Philip With The Glasses. And I had begun to understand how things worked. And one of the things I understood is that if The People are presented with a choice of things that are more or less the same they will go for the one that looks best.

And this made me think.

Be Ruthless
If you want the Revolution to succeed you have to Be Ruthless.

And this made me think too.

Seizure The Moment

And then Mr Smith who was the Leader of the Labour Party had a heart attack and died.

So I did a really good Ovation about what a Great Man Mr Smith had been. And what a Great Prime Minister he would have surely become. And I did the Ovation because Gordon was too upset to speak because Mr Smith had been a Close Friend of his.

And then I told Gordon that actually I should be Leader and Not Him.

And I told him that even Peter who had always been Gordon's best friend agreed. And so did Alastair. And so did Philip With The Glasses. And so did Anji.

And That Was That.

So that's how I became Leader Of The Labour Party.

What Alastair Said After Reading This Last Bit

What Alastair said after reading this last bit was: 'I think you should change this last bit.'

And I said, 'Why?'

And he said, 'I don't think it shows you in a very good light.'

And I said, 'Why?'

And he said, 'Well, you come across as Being Ruthless.'

And I said, 'I wasn't Being Ruthless. I was Making A Tough Decision.'

And Alastair said, 'Tony, mate, it's me you're talking to. Describe it how you like, but we all know that you shafted Gordon.'

And I was shocked. Because I'm not that kind of

person. And Gordon is not only a far cleverer man than me whom I Admire And Respect In So Many Ways but also a Close Personal Friend. And I only put myself forward ahead of him because it was for The Good Of The Party. And Of The Country.

When I explained all this to Alastair he did a look that means: 'I hear the totality of what you're saying and whilst I acknowledge that there are many valid points in your line of reasoning I remain unconvinced.'

It was a look that was very similar to his 'Bollocks!' look.

Granita

In the end Gordon agreed about me being Leader. But he wasn't happy. So I thought that the best way to make him happy was if I spent a lot of time with him Discussing Things.

We met lots and lots and lots. We were doing something called Thrashing Out An Agreement. This is where you each start off with Your Own Agreement and then Thrash Them Out until in the end there's only one agreement left. And then instead of each having your own agreement you end up with one agreement between the Two Of You. And then you can go home.

Except we didn't go home because Gordon was still a bit glum about it all. So I said I'd take him out to dinner. There was a fab new and Very Trendy restaurant in Islington that everyone was talking about called Granita that I'd wanted to go to for ages which Gordon had never heard of.

We had a lovely dinner. (Though Gordon couldn't have been that hungry because he didn't eat anything.) And Gordon thinks we finally did A Deal.

In Gordon's Deal he would not fight me over The

Leadership if he could be in charge of things like The Economy and Social Policy and Making The Country Fairer. Then I could be Prime Minister, get to meet The Queen and some Celebrities, and be in charge of Foreign Policy. And if I was in charge of Foreign Policy that means I could go on holiday a lot to Tuscany which would be good because by now me and Cherry had A Large And Happy Family.*

The menus came and the menus looked great, so as I was reading mine I was nodding a lot. Gordon was talking about how he could Take Over The Reins in seven years but I wasn't really listening because I was so busy reading the menu.

Gordon kept on talking and because I hadn't really been listening I did the nodding my head and saying 'Yes' very slowly (which is also really useful when you're not that interested in what is going on). And by the time he was finished talking I was Really Hungry. So I said, 'Shall we order, then?'

And we did.

Later that night I asked Cherry what a Granita was and she said it was a dish that was actually just grated ice but with a sweet syrup poured over it to make it tasty so that you never realise that all you are eating is only frozen water.

I said that I'd really liked the restaurant and that it had been a great place to sort out what Gordon could do whilst I was doing being Prime Minister. And also to sort out The Future Of the Labour Party.

---

*This is another reason why it was for the Best All Round if I became Leader and not Gordon as he Did Not Have A Family†.
†This is *not* a euphemism. And I always told this to all the people who suggested that it is. And so has everyone on my team.

One Of The Best Things About Being Leader

One of the Best Things about being Leader is making lots of speeches. I like making speeches. My favourite speeches are ones that are full of Important Ideas And Initiatives.

The best way to put across an Important Idea And Initiative, especially to The People, is with a Soundbite. A lot of people think I do too many Soundbites and that this is a Bad Thing. But I think that Soundbites are part of the job. And that criticising me for doing Soundbites would be like criticising me for turning up for bed in pyjamas.*

I have done lots of Soundbites. Here are some of my best ones:

1   Education. Education. Education.
2   We are on your side: your ambitions are our ambitions … We are on your side: your concerns are our concerns … We are on your side: your aspirations are our aspirations.†
3   We are The People's Party.
4   New Labour, Eternal Values.
5   New Labour, New Britain.
6   Tough on crime, tough on the causes of crime.
7   The Third Way.
8   No more sleaze. No more lies. No more broken promises.
9   Leadership, not drift.

---

*This is a good example of a Soundbite.

†Ambitions and aspirations are more or less the same thing (I think) but repeating something three times is good for The Rhythm and Adds Emphasis. For instance if in Soundbite 1 I'd said 'Education. Education. Top Up Fees', it wouldn't have been such a good Soundbite or such a good speech.

10 The future, not the past.

11 I want us to be a young country again.

12 Freedom. Responsibility. Family. Efficiency. These are Labour words.

13 I am worth no more than anyone else.*

14 I am my brother's keeper.

15 I will not walk by on the other side.

16 I am the Way, the Truth and the Light.

17 This is our Dome. Britain's Dome, and believe me it will be the Envy Of The World.

Actually, now I come to think about it more, Sound-bites aren't really like Riffs in rock songs, they're more like the catchiest line in a pop song (or Hook as we say). That's because both use Words.

This is an example of a very famous Hook from a very successful pop song.

La la la,
La la, la-lah lah
La la la,
La la, la-lah la

It is 'Can't Get You Out Of My Head' by Kylie. So in a Hook it's not what the words actually say that really matters, but the *feeling* that it conveys.

And a Soundbite is just the same.

---

*I try not to do this Soundbite when Gordon can hear because it makes him cross.

New Labour

This was another Good Idea of ours. We thought of it because we were Modernisers. And because we were modernising the Old Labour Party.

Philip With The Glasses was very keen on changing the name. That's because he was an 'ad-man' and knew all about Brands. He said we had to Shift Perception Of Our Brand. We had to dispel the old Bad Things people thought about Labour. These are some of those things:

Bad Things

Pals with trade unions
Strikes
Bad with money
Always arguing
Don't like business
Blame society for crime
Beards
Don't like middle classes
Do like raising taxes and spending the money on daft
    schemes
Bad suits

And we all agreed that we could change the name because We Had Changed. And we would Go On Changing as circumstances evolved. But we also agreed that this was OK because the values at the Centre Of Our Being would always remain the same.

This is because we all had Irreducible Cores. And what's more we all had the same Irreducible Core which was great.

Irreducible Cores was one of My Best Ideas.

So that's why it was OK for us to change the name of The Labour Party.

But changing the name of an Institution Steeped In As Much History as The Labour Party was not a Decision We Took Lightly. Here are some of the names we thought about:

Improved Labour
Labour Plus
Laboure
Labour Moderne
Labour!
Totally Labour
Everything You Wanted From Labour But Were Afraid
    To Ask
We're Labour, Are You?
The People's Labour
Your Labour
Your Labour Because You're Labour
Labour And You
It's A Labour Thing
Labour, Labour, Labour!
Consignia
I Can't Believe We're Not Tories

But in the end we chose New Labour.

The Brand Thing

This is one of the things Philip With The Glasses was really good at. Because he had been an 'ad-man'. So he knew how to sell things. And how to sell things in a Competitive Marketplace where most people weren't sure if they wanted to buy anything and most products were more or less the same anyway.

He drew a diagram. This is that diagram.

THE BRAND

THE BRAND'S CORE VALUES

THE BRAND MESSAGE

THE PRODUCT

THE FEATURES OF THE PRODUCT THAT BEST
REPRESENT THE BRAND'S CORE VALUES

THE PRODUCT MESSAGE

THE COHERENT DELIVERY OF THE PRODUCT
MESSAGE THAT BOTH DRAWS ON AND
STRENGTHENS THE BRAND MESSAGE AND IS
CONSISTENT ACROSS ALL AREAS OF
COMMUNICATION

⇩

THE CONSUMER

I didn't really understand it. So I just shook my head
slowly and said 'Yes'.

But Alastair was very excited. He said, 'This is why we'll
fuck the Tories. Major* thinks the secret is about traipsing

---

*Mr Major had become Prime Minister after Mrs Thatcher. His
best idea was The Cones Hotline. I secretly always liked this idea.
But I always joined in when the others laughed about it.

around the country and climbing up on a soap box, when the secret is actually about Becoming The Soap!'

For a while Alastair worked on a cracking idea called 'The New Labour Doorstep Challenge'. But in the end he couldn't get Danny Baker so he decided against it.

Alastair Makes Another Comment

When Alastair read all this he really enjoyed it because he was in it a lot. But then he made another comment. This is the comment he made:

'Tony, we still seem to be a long way from Iraq.'

And I said, 'Alastair, it's All Relevant.'

And he said, 'How?'

And I said, 'Well, take that last diagram that Philip With The Glasses did. What if I was The Brand, and The War was The Product.'

And he said, 'That's quite clever.'

And I said, 'I am quite clever.'

Analogies And How They Work

Alastair says an Analogy is a way of explaining complex ideas by saying that the complex idea is like something simpler so that people who are too busy can understand the complex idea. When Alastair says 'busy' he makes The Bunny Ears Sign. The Bunny Ears Sign is nothing to do with bunnies. Or their ears.

Alastair uses Analogies a lot when he explains things to me. And so does Peter. And so does Philip With The Glasses. And so does Cherry when she's teaching me about cooking. Or when we are in our bedroom doing sex.*

This is an Analogy that Alastair thought of:

Elections are a bit like The World Cup. But a World Cup in which the England team gets picked by someone who in the years between World Cup

---

*But sometimes with Cherry I do get confused. Like when she decided she Wanted Another Baby and started talking about trains and tunnels. And I explained to her that it Wasn't That Simple because there was Railtrack and Network Rail and the Train Operating Companies and Jarvis and The Strategic Rail Authority Which Really Was A Good Idea But Had Run Its Course to consider. And she said, 'I love it when you talk dirty.' But I didn't understand what she meant. So I said, 'Let me just ask Anji about all this because she's good on "knowing what women like".' And then Cherry must have changed her mind because she got up and went downstairs and decided to chat to her pal Carole on the telephone for ages. Luckily Carole is on our 'Friends & Family' list which really keeps the bills down.

*tournaments isn't actually interested in football,
and doesn't go to matches, or even watch it on TV,
but just because they know the music for Match Of
The Day they think they know what they're talking
about.*

Alastair liked this Analogy a lot because it linked
politics to football. And politics and football are Alastair's
two favourite things.

And then Alastair Extended His Analogy.

Alastair said that when there was an Election his job
really was:

*To be a pundit in the studio explaining to people
what to expect before the game, explain how it's
going at half time, and explain after the game is over
why we won the match whatever the score actually
was.*

So that's what Alastair taught me about Presentation.

An Analogy Of My Own

But I wanted to show Alastair that I had understood the
way he'd explained Presentation to me. So I Thought Of
My Own Analogy. And My Analogy is much cleverer than
his because it actually has the word 'present' in it which
is the first part of the word Presentation.

This is the Analogy I thought of:

*Presentation is a bit like when you give someone a
present on their birthday and put it in a lovely box
and wrap it in lovely paper and tie it up with a lovely
ribbon and put a lovely card on it so when you give
it to them they will be really happy because you've*

taken so much care with the present's Present-
ation.

When I told Alastair My Analogy he said, 'And they won't actually notice until long after the party is over and everyone has gone home that the present inside is actually crap.'

And then he laughed, though I don't know why.

But there was no time to dwell on it because there was An Election coming.

Bambi Bites Back

Even though I was the best person to be Prime Minister some of the newspapers didn't think so. They thought I was too soft and cuddly. That's why they called me The Trendy Vicar. And some even started calling me Bambi.

Bambi was a lovely baby deer in a Walter Disney film called *Bambi*.

I liked being called Bambi because it meant people thought I was lovely. (Which I was.) But Peter pointed out a problem with this. The problem Peter pointed out was this:

'Are you too lovely to take hard and ruthless decisions?'

I said I wasn't. And Gordon agreed.

And then we all agreed that I needed to Project A New Image for the Media.

So we sat down and tried to come up with a new image. And that's when Peter had a brainwave. This is what he said:

'What we need to do is change Bambi into Rambo.'

So I said, 'How do we do that?'

And Alastair said, 'That's easy. All we need is a War. And then you need to go in and rescue someone. And you probably need to start going down the gym.'

War: What Is It Good For?
But Alastair was Only Joking because even I knew you can't decide to do a War by yourself just because you want to and for reasons that you never really explain.

So we decided to do a War On Something.

And three of the things we decided to do a War On

80

was Old Labour and The Power Of The Unions Within The Labour Party and Crime.*

Something That I Am Very Good At (Besides Acting And Toast)

Something that I am very good at (besides acting and toast) is knowing what to do when people die.

When people die you must do these four things:

1 Wear a dark suit.
2 Look sad.
3 Catch the mood of the nation.
4 Quietly seize the opportunity to advance your agenda.

Most politicians understand point one and point two. But no one understands point three and point four as well as I do. That's yet another reason why I am the best person to be Prime Minister and they are not.

It's also because sometimes I am very good at Analysing Things. Analysing Things is when you Think Very Hard about something. And when you Think Very Hard about something you can often come up with a Useful Insight.

When I Thought Very Hard about what happens when people die I realised that:

---

*And later on we decided to do a War on Drugs. And later on we decided to do a War On Terrorism. And later on we decided to do a War On Bogus Asylum Seekers. And later on we decided to do a War On Mr Hussein. And later on we decided to do a War On The BBC. And later on we decided to do a War On Anything That Lots Of People Thought Was Bad.

1 People are Sad.
2 People are Emotional.
3 People are Not Rational.
4 People want someone to say, 'There, there, don't worry, it'll be all right.'

And my best Useful Insight was that if someone says, 'There, there, don't worry, it'll be all right' to The People when they are Sad and Emotional and Not Rational it is easy to go on to say, 'And it doesn't have to be just all right. It can be better.'

This is because when people die, the people who didn't die want Hope. And if you give them Hope they will warm to you. And if they warm to you they are more likely to vote for you at Elections.

And this is what I did when these people died:

1 Mr Smith
2 Jamie

And much later

3 The people in the Twin Towers

Jamie was a small boy from The North who was murdered by two other boys. I did a Speech about it. It was about Being Tough On Crime.

And people thought about me differently after that. And people stopped calling me A Trendy Vicar. And people stopped calling me Bambi.

But my best Knowing What To Do When People Die was after Princess Diana was killed in an accidental car accident.

A Candle In The Wind

The whole nation was shocked when Princess Diana died. They needed someone to speak for them. So I did. I explained that we were all so shocked because she was 'The People's Princess'. It was a phrase that truly summed up what I felt.

Alastair had suggested it. And it really Caught The Mood Of The Nation. In fact, it was my best Catching The Mood Of The Nation.

And when her family and The Queen wanted a small private funeral me and Alastair said, 'No, let's have a Big Funeral. That way everyone can be a part of it.' And when I talked to Charles, who was her husband but had split up from her and thought he would be the King one day, he agreed.

And one of the best things about having a Big Funeral was that everyone would be able to see how sad everyone else was.

So we had a Big Funeral. And me and Alastair advised The Queen on The Media and what to do about it all so that she wouldn't be Seen In A Bad Light.

Everyone agrees that I handled things really well. This means that even in This Hour Of Tragedy I was Seen In A Good Light. And everyone warmed to me even more. My approval rating soared to over 90 per cent. I became The Most Popular Prime Minister Since Records Began.

A candle in the wind

But all that happened later. First we had to Win The Election.

How We Won The Election And Changed The Face Of History In Britain

When Alastair read the title of this chapter he said this:

'Tony, I think you ought to change the title of this chapter.'

And I said, 'Why?'

And he said, 'I think it comes across as a bit Big Headed.'

And I said, 'But it's true.'

And he said, 'Yes, I know it's true and you know it's true but "humble" plays better with The People.'

And I said, 'You mean like when we did a Landslide at the election and Behind Closed Doors were all jumping up and down and high fiving and whooping and ordering the 15-inch pizzas with lots of extra toppings and not worrying about the cost despite what Gordon said and hitting that picture of Mr Major with our shoes and pretending to fart in the direction of Tory Central Office and spraying very expensive champagne over everyone like Mr Ecclestone's car drivers and then stripping off to just our underpants and putting our arms round each other and singing "We Are The Champions, My Friend" at the top of our voices, but then putting on a Serious And Responsible face and going out to tell The People that "We Were The Servants Now"?'

And Alastair said, 'Yes.'

So I changed the title.

This is the new title:

How I Was Given A Very Large And Utterly Priceless Bowl And Had To Walk Miles And Miles Down Slippery Passageways Without Dropping It

Alastair read this new title and said, 'What does it mean?'

And I said, 'I don't really know. But my friend Roy With The Funny Rs said it. And he said it was about me and the election. And if I put it in the book maybe someone will explain it to me.'

And Alastair said, 'No, that's not a good title either.'

So I said, 'Well, why don't you think of a title then?'

And he said, 'OK, I will.'

And he did.

And it was a good title. And I was about to use Alastair's title when A Thought Occurred To Me and I said, 'But, Alastair, this is supposed to be *my* book and if I let you write the title of this chapter then you'll be Putting Words In My Mouth and people might get the Wrong Idea that all I am is the Good Looking Spokesman.'

And Alastair said, 'No, Tony. You mustn't think that. You're the Prime Minister. I'm just here to help you. I mean, how can I have so much influence and power when I haven't even been elected? That just wouldn't be democratic. Obviously I'm just "a servant" too.'

And I said, 'You mean "a Servant of The People", just like me?'

And he said, 'Yeah. Exactly like that.'

And he smiled so he must have been happy.

And when he explained it to me like that I could see that it was all OK. So I used his title.

From Revolution To War

Our best idea was to fight the Election like a War. We knew it was our best idea because we had got it from my friend Bill in America who was The President back then.

Philip With The Glasses had gone and done a sleepover while Bill was fighting his Election.* They were having an Election because they too are A Democracy. And being A Democracy is the best and fairest way to run a country which is why we're Bringing Democracy to Iraq.†

Philip With The Glasses was very excited when he came back. He was so excited that he wrote a short memo about it all. It was only 712 pages.

When the others finished reading the memo we all sat around and punched the air and said American things like:

'Hell, yeah!'

'Let's roll!'

'Let's kick ass!'

'Let freedom reign!'

'No sleep till Downing Street!'

and

'Talk to the press release, coz the politician ain't listening!'

Then we put on a Bruce Springsteen record and we

---

*At this point Alastair said, 'Shouldn't that read "Bill was fighting his erection"?' And I said 'No.' And Alastair said, 'Sorry, you're right. He won when he fought his election, then he lost when he fought his erection!' Then he laughed a lot.

†Curiously, in some countries Democracy is not a good idea. Like Saudi Arabia. These countries are often called Allies Of The West.

all danced about and all sang along. And we drank Bud-weisers.*

Bruce Springsteen is also called The Boss. I tried to get the others to call me The Boss. And they all did. But for some reason they always did The Bunny Ears sign when they did. I explained to them that this Wasn't Appropriate. And they all said 'OK'. But they all did The Bunny Ears Sign again when they said 'OK'. So I Gave Up.

The song we all sang was called 'Born To Run'.

It was Very Appropriate.

The Nine Commandments Of Campaigning

This was another of our Good Ideas. It helped us Be Clear about what The War we were fighting was like. These are the Nine Commandments.

1. **Campaigning is Holistic.** Holistic is a funny word. It is nothing to do with holes. It is to do with everything. A better spelling would be 'wholistic'. Then it would be easier to understand. What we decided was that every-thing that happens and everything you do and everything you say and how you do it and say it in whatever medium, is part of the Campaign.

2. **Campaigning is Dynamic.** This is like in Batman. He was part of the Dynamic Duo. This means that things happened and he dealt with them. Some of the things he knew would happen, and some of them he didn't. But he dealt with both of these types of things.

3. **Campaigning is about Momentum.** In a Campaign

---

*True.

you are either gaining Momentum or you are losing Momentum. There is no Third Way.*

4. **Campaigning is about Speed.** Speed is about acting quickly. It is *not* about Gary Speed who is a football player who played for Leeds United and Newcastle United and Wales United.

5. **Campaigning is about Not Giving Up.** Campaigns go on and on and on and on. They are Relentless. So you need stamina. That's why we ate lots of bananas.

6. **Campaigning is about Trust.** Trust is very important for The Electorate. (The Electorate is what The People are called when there is an Election.) The Electorate want to

---

*I didn't really Understand what Momentum meant. So one evening when me and Cherry were trying to Make Another Baby I asked her what 'momentum' was. And she sighed and said, 'Well, you've just lost it.' And went to make a cup of Sainsbury's Taste The Difference Camomile And Ginseng Tea and have a chat with her friend Carole on the phone. And when she came back I said, 'Cherry, I don't understand.' And she drank her tea and explained it to me. And after she had explained it to me I still didn't understand so I stared at the word really hard and then A Light Bulb Came On. (A light bulb didn't really come on. This is just a Colourful Colloquial Expression. Colourful Colloquial Expressions are useful when you make a speech because they make the audience think that you are On Their Wavelength. My best most recent Colourful Colloquial Expression was in a 'debate' in the House Of Commons where I sometimes go to have tea. I said, 'Mr Hussein? Weapons Of Mass Destruction? South of the River, this time of night? Are you Havin' A Larf?' It was a big success.)

be able to trust the politicians they elect to be The Government. If they do trust the politicians they elect to be The Government then they can Get On With Their Lives and not have to worry about the things that are being Done In Their Name.

7. **Campaigning is about Beating Fear.** This is especially true when you are In Opposition. And have been for a very long time. That's because The Government will try to make The Electorate afraid of what you would do if you won The Election and become The Government. So you have to Beat The Fear. And create Hope.*

8. **Campaigning is about Substance.** There has to be something inside the soap box.

9. **Campaigning is about Being On Message.** There are two types of Message. There is The Big Message that is your central line of reasoning why The Electorate should Vote For You. Then there are The Small Messages that are about specific things or issues that support and strengthen The Big Message. That's why it's important that you're always On Message.

I liked having Commandments. That's because Commandments make it easy to understand what is Right and Wrong. And I believe in Right and Wrong.

They have Commandments in The Bible which is my

---

*But when you have been The Government for A Long Time you have to Change Sides. That's because it's hard to sell Hope when you've been running things for ages. So when you've been In Power for A Long Time campaigning is about creating Fear.

best favourite book. This is one of the Commandments in The Bible:

Thou Shalt Not Kill.

In many ways when you are Prime Minister this is quite a tricky Commandment. But luckily when I Looked Deep Into My Soul I realised that it doesn't apply all the time. And that when Moses came down from the mountain with the Commandments on The Tablets Of Stone he had left behind by mistake some of the Caveats that God had originally included, and so The People had ended up being misled as to the exact intentions of The Commandments. But after he had held an inquiry God realised that it had been nobody's fault and had been more of a Collective Failing and so no one was to blame or had to be sent to Hell.

But the thing I did know about Commandments is that there should be Ten. So I said, 'Hey, guys. There should be Ten Commandments.'

And this made everyone Stop and Think. And what everyone decided that we needed was one Commandment that was the Central Commandment. The one Commandment that summed up everything we would do and everything that we stood for.

But no one knew what it should be. So I looked at my Bible for Inspiration and realised that a lot of The Commandments started 'Thou shalt not …'

'A lot of The Commandments in The Bible start "Thou shalt not …", ' I said. And that inspired Alastair and he said, in a God-like voice:

'THOU SHALT NOT LOSE!'

And everyone liked it a lot so it became our Tenth Commandment.

Before long everyone started calling it our Number Ten Commandment.

But no-one explained to me why they did this.

Some Of The Other Ways That We Increased The Scale Of Our Operation And Its 'Sophistication'

I like the word 'Sophistication'. It means cleverness and complexity. I like it because it sounds like it should have an 'f' in it, but it doesn't. I like things that Might Not Be What They Seem to be at first glance. And I like words that turn out to be different from how you expect them to be at first listen.

Millbank

One of the first ways that we increased the scale and sophistication of our operation was by getting a new place to work.

Millbank was the name of our new offices. Millbank was lovely and it was modern. And since we were Modernisers and I was lovely this was appropriate. Instead of there being lots of small meeting rooms and corridors you got lost in there was one Big Room where everyone could sit together in Perfect Harmony.

Peter used to hate the small rooms and 'labyrinthine' corridors of our old offices. He said that they were 'Symptomatic of the Old Labour Mindset'. He called them 'The Corridors Of Lack Of Power' which is a very clever 'play on words'. But he was used to being in small rooms and 'labyrinthine' corridors, that's why he's such a tough fighter and good at working in very tight corners. But now he preferred to play in The Big Room.

The War Room

Except we didn't call it The Big Room. We called it The War Room. Calling it The War Room gave it a sense of purpose. And a feeling of camaraderie. Camaraderie means all being in something together. Another word for this feeling is Community which is something I've always believed in. I believe when a Community acts together it can achieve Great Things.*

We'd got the idea for The War Room from my friend Bill in America. And also from Big Business. Big Businesses often have 'open plan' offices. And the best thing about this is that everyone can talk to each other really easily because everyone's plans seem to be in the open. And Momentum is easier to generate and to maintain.

But just because we had a lovely new 'open plan' War Room we weren't going to forget our Fundamental Principles. So The Inner Core still made all the important decisions. And although we didn't make them openly, the new offices made it look like we were making them in the open. This was good because it gave everyone else The Illusion Of Involvement. And this also helped generate energy.

In A War Good Intelligence Is Vital

If you don't have Good Intelligence in a War you can lose everything. You can end up fighting the wrong battles, at the wrong time, in the wrong place, with the wrong

---

*But sometimes when a Community acts together it can Get Things Wrong. Like when all those people marched against The War. That's why it's best to have someone in charge of The Community who decides if The Community is doing the right thing.

weapons, against the wrong enemy and for the wrong reasons.

That's why Media Monitoring is so important.

And why we had a computer called Excalibur. Excalibur's job was to read all the newspaper articles, press releases and documents relating to the Election and file the information away in its memory so that The Troops could access the Relevant Data at the press of a button. It was fantastic. It was just like Hal in the movie *2001: A Space Odyssey*.

And then, once you've got the information, you have to use it.

The Attack Task Force

This was a task force dedicated to attacking the enemy. If you attack at the right time with the right resources you do one of the most important things: you Set The Agenda. If you can Set The Agenda then you have chosen the Battle Ground. And the enemy will be Forced Onto The Back Foot and has to defend itself.

One of the best ways to make sure that you Set The Agenda is to always enter the News Cycle at the earliest possible moment. To do this you must have good relations with the Media, so how you see the Media is very important.

How We Saw The Media

Some people say that the Media is a beast but it's not. I realised this one day when I was looking after my teenage children Mick and Marianne* while I let Cherry have a go at running the country for a change.

The Media is not like a beast. The Media is more like

---

*Baby Keef hadn't been born yet.

a Teenager. It needs constant feeding, it needs constant pandering to and it gets bored of things easily. It doesn't like having to think too hard and it likes to feel that it's always at the cutting edge. And despite its rebellious appearance, deep down it really, really wants to fit in. And if you can make it feel that it can be in on something new and fresh and young and that's going to win then it's easy to get the Media on your side.

So we did all that. We went up to its bedroom, knocked on its door and passed in endless toasted sandwiches. And we let it stay up late and watch whatever it wanted on 'the box'. And the real secret of winning the Media over is the same as winning a teenager over. Just treat it like a grown-up. Or pretend to. And that's how The Super Soaraway *Sun* became our New Best Mate.

The Rapid Rebuttal Unit

This is the other side of the coin. You have to repel an enemy attack as soon as it happens. So you need the facts and figures instantly available to counter any story the enemy generates. That way their stories can never gain Momentum. And they constantly have to generate new lines of attack because they can't sustain any advance they make. And that is very tiring. And in the end the enemy attacks become less and less believable and less and less effective.

It was all very exciting. I spent a lot of time humming the theme to *633 Squadron* as I sat in the meetings trying to keep up with what was being decided. Or sometimes it was the theme to *The Dam Busters.* (And recently I seem to be humming the theme to *The Great Escape* quite a lot.)

The Third Side Of The Coin

This is a very peculiar heading because coins don't have a third side. They have heads and they have tails, though not in the same way that animals have them. But if you take a coin and flick it up into the air it will spin and spin and spin. And if you watch it closely as it spins it's hard to tell if what you're looking at is the head or the tail.* That's because the movement has created an illusion of something else. Something that is not the head or the tail but something that in the blur of its action is somehow more desirable than either.

And that's what Spinning is. And that's why I think of Spin as the third side of the coin. It is not the head and it is not the tail. It is neither attack nor defence. It is a blurring of both. This is the best way to deal with the Media.

Alastair is the best at doing Spinning. You might think that Spinning is most useful during an Election. It isn't. It's after the Election when you are In Power that Spinning works best to help you make the country A Better Place.

Alastair explained to me that during an Election The People watch what goes on a bit more closely. So while the Spinning coin will distract them for a while if they keep their eyes on it they will eventually see it fall to the ground. But after the Election they are too busy with their own lives. So spin enough coins and they'll be so distracted and confused about where to look next that they'll never see any of them hit the ground.

---

*Although it's easier to tell the difference with most animals. Except small rodents.

A spinning coin

The other way to look at Spinning is that it's just another form of advertising. You take something that's happened or is about to happen and portray it in its best possible light. Or the light that best serves your purpose. Which is what everybody does.

One of Alastair's Best Ideas when it came to Spinning was to cultivate a group of journalists who he would Let In On Things. This made them feel that they were Close To The Action. And if they felt this then it was easier for them to see Our Side Of The Story.

(This was such a Good Idea that when we were doing War with Mr Hussein we even let journalists be Embedded with Our Forces. 'Embedded' is nothing to do with doing sex, although Alastair did say 'The great thing about embedding journalists is that it fucks up their objectivity'.)

Focus Groups

This was another of Philip With The Glasses's ideas. A Focus Group is a bit like an opinion poll but it goes into things in More Depth. Instead of stopping someone when they're out shopping in the high street and it looks like it's just about to rain and asking them what they think about something, you invite them in after work, sit them on a sofa, give them a glass of Chardonnay and some expensive crisps and ask them in a supportive way what they *really* think about something.

Obviously the answers you get are much more meaningful.

And at the end of it Philip With The Glasses writes up everything and interprets it for you and puts it in a report and gives it to you. And that way you have Inside Information that no one else has and you can learn What Is Really Going On and What People Are Really Thinking and you can Act Accordingly.

A Popular Misconception About Focus Groups

A popular misconception about Focus Groups is that we use them so that we can find out what people think and want and then decide on what policies to do, but that's not how Focus Groups work. That's because we are More Sophisticated Than That. Focus Groups tell us what people think so that we can go away and look at our policies and decide which bits of our policies to talk about. And we discover the bits of our policies that the Focus Groups aren't interested in or actually dislike and then make the sensible decision not to talk about these bits.

The other thing that everyone misses about Focus Groups is that it's not what you focus on that's most important, but who you focus on. So in the lead-up to the Election we mostly focused on 'Conservative voters who were considering switching to Labour'.

This is A Quite Considerable Insight into how a modern democracy works especially during an Election.

Know Yourself

The last piece of Intelligence you need to fight an Election is not about The Enemy. And it's not about The People. It's about You. You have to know your strengths. And, more importantly, you have to know your weaknesses.

All this stuff about Intelligence is a bit confusing. So I've thought of some pictures to help explain it.

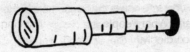

Know the Enemy

Know The People

Know Yourself

What You Do After You've Done All This Stuff

What you do after you've done all this stuff is come up with The Plan. The Plan has to be comprehensive, coherent and both firm and flexible. And then you stick to The Plan.

Do that and, as Philip With The Glasses used to say, you can turn something complicated, multi-layered and dynamic into simple, sustainable, communicable truths and that's what influences the consumers in their decision to buy at the point of purchase.

It all sounded Very Clever. And it worked.

So we did all these things. And that's how we Won The Election.

What Alastair Thought About All This

I showed all this to Alastair to see what he thought.

'What do you think, Alastair?' I said.

He said, 'I like the bits with me in it.'

And I said, 'What about the other bits?'

And he said, 'Well, I suppose they've got to be in there.'

And I said, 'Yes, they have.'

And he said, 'It was great when we won. And we didn't just win, we had a fucking great landslide!'

And I said, 'Yes, it was great.'

And he said, 'The funny thing is no one spotted that the problem with a landslide is that afterwards someone has to clear up the mess.'

And he laughed. But I didn't know what he meant.

And then he said, 'Tone, mate, dog's bollocksy though all this election stuff is, are you sure that it's relevant to the War in Iraq? I mean, isn't that what this book is supposed to be about?'

And I said, 'Don't worry, because I've worked all that out too.'

And he said, 'Go on.'

And I said, 'Alastair, look, we did such good election wins because we *ran the Election Campaign like a War*. And that's why when had to do War with Mr Hussein the only sensible thing to do was *run the War like an Election Campaign.*'

And when you Understand This, You Understand Everything.

And Alastair said, 'You mean like we did with Kosovo?'

And I said, 'Yes, like we did with Kosovo.'

Kosovo

Kosovo used to be part of Yugoslavia. But in 1999 it was part of Serbia. And the man in charge of Serbia was Mr Milosevic. Mr Milosevic was a very bad man. He was a Tyrant and a Dictator. And he was doing Ethnic Cleansing on some of the people he ruled who were Kosovan Albanians.

So lots of the Kosovan Albanians were deciding to be refugees.*

I wanted to help These Poor People. And Stop Their Persecution. The UN were involved and so were NATO. But no one was taking a lead. And no one was making Mr Milosevic think that we meant business. So he was just carrying on.

Before I had been Prime Minister the International Community including Britain had done Too Little, Too Late to stop the bloodshed in Bosnia and Croatia. I wasn't going to let this happen again in Kosovo.

So I took the lead.

And so did the Americans.

We bombed Mr Milosevic's forces. The bombing was very smart but it was not a success. And Mr Milosevic

---

*I like helping refugees. They are people whose 'situation in their own country has become intolerable and who need our sympathy and our charity and not our condemnation'. I especially like helping refugees in mainland Europe and Africa. Curiously, when refugees get to Britain they sometimes stop being refugees and become Bogus Asylum Seekers who are out to fleece us and our generous system. When that happens I have to set David With The Dog on them.

used it as an excuse to drive out more Kosovan Albanians.

I realised that the only solution was to send in Ground Forces. I said we'd send in 50,000 men. Which would have been just about everyone, from everywhere, who wasn't already busy. But my friend Bill didn't want to send any men in.

So I had to Force His Hand. Just by coincidence right then stories appeared in The News Media in the UK and in America where Bill lived saying that Bill was 'being a wuss'. I have no idea where these stories came from. And neither does Alastair.

Shortly after that Bill said he was thinking about sending in Ground Forces. And then Mr Milosevic gave up and stopped doing Ethnic Cleansing.

What Alastair Did To Help With All This

What Alastair did to help with all this was to go to Brussels to show NATO how to do Media. After he got there they did Spin and Rapid Rebuttal, Being On Message, Embedding Stories, Press Conferences, Setting The Agenda and Undermining The Enemy Within.

He was brilliant.

How I Invented A Historic Doctrine

In the middle of all this I had to do a Speech in Chicago. I wanted to make it a Big and Important Speech about what I believed about International Affairs.

But I had been so busy that I hadn't been able to think about what I believed.

So I asked a friend of a friend what he believed. And he came up with Five Criteria For Principled Intervention. And when I read them I realised that luckily this was what I believed too. These are the Five Criteria For Principled Intervention:

1 Are we sure of our case?
2 Have all diplomatic options been exhausted?
3 Can we expect the military to succeed?
4 Are we prepared for the long term?
5 Are our national interests really involved?*

On the flight over to Chicago I had already seen the film that they were showing so I decided to write down some of my own own thoughts. And that's when I remembered how ever since I was at Uni I had thought that Community had been important, so why shouldn't we see things in terms of The International Community where everyone acted together to make everything lovely for everyone, all the time, and where Bad Leaders and Rogue States

---

*These Five Criteria were very useful later on when we had to do a War on Mr Hussein because I looked at them and I decided that they had all been clearly met. That's how I knew that our Intervention was Principled.

were sorted out by the other members of The International Community?

And that's how I came up with my very own Doctrine. And I called my Doctrine 'The Doctrine Of The International Community'. And the Speech was a big hit. And everyone clapped. (Well, all except The Foreign Office and their lawyers. And I didn't really listen to them anyway.)

The Chicago Speech was very, very important. Especially to me. And to how I saw My Role In The World. But because I made it in Chicago not many people in Britain realised just how Serious I Was About It All.

Things I Learned From Kosovo
I learned that I was Tough. And Principled. And that I could be an International Leader. And that I was willing to take Hard Decisions. And that sometimes I have to help the US come to the Right Conclusions. And that wars could be fought and won like Election Campaigns.

And that I had My Very Own Doctrine.*

Something That Occurred To Me Quite Recently
Something that occurred to me quite recently is that while it is great having invented a Doctrine all the top leaders that I most admire had a word named after them. Mrs

---

*When I got home and told Cherry about how I had invented my 'Doctrine Of The International Community' and asked her what she thought about it she said, 'It's very nice, dear,' and went back to watching Heartbeat.

So I said, 'Cherry, I don't think you realise how important and world changing My New Doctrine is.' And she said, 'Anthony, you can't just declare a doctrine of The International Community on your own. I think you'll find that if you really want it to work

Thatcher has got Thatcherism, Mr Reagan had Reagonomics, Mr Churchill had Churchillian and the Marx Brothers had Marxism. But I hadn't got anything.

So I asked Alastair to come up with some choices. Having choices is always important. That's why in our new improved National Health Service everyone will have lots of choices so they will be bound to get a better service.

This is the list Alastair came up with:

Blairism
Blairgonomics
Blairite
Blairist
Blairful
Blairy

I didn't like the list. I told Alastair I didn't like the list. None of them sounded very nice. None of them sounded like me. And I realised that if this was a project that was really going to succeed I would have to Take Charge Of It Myself. The other thing I realised was that the fundamental flaw in Alastair's list was that it used my surname. But ever since I had become Prime Minister and run my first Cabinet I had said to everyone 'Call me Tony'.

---

you have to first ask the other members of "The International Community" whether they want to be in "The International Community" and on what terms. And aren't you just doing what you always do: inventing the whole concept of "The International Community" as a post-rationalisation of a decision you have already taken?'

But I think she was just annoyed because I was interrupting her watching Nick Berry in a uniform.

This was to make everyone Feel At Ease, and as if we were All Mates, and that we were All Equal.

This is my list:

Tonyism
Tonified
Toniful
Tonetastic
TonicalafragalisticexpealiBlairtious

I gave the list to Alastair and asked if he could subtly start dropping the words into all Government press releases.

He was so excited at the prospect that he said, 'Fucking hell, Tone,' and dropped his mug of Bovril.

Only Me!
One of the Best Things about having come up with the Doctrine Of The International Community was that because it was all about Foreign Policy I didn't have to talk to Gordon about it. And, even better, in Foreign Policy the issues were Black & White. In Foreign Policy you could adopt a Moral Position.*

---

*The Moral Position I chose to adopt on most Foreign Policy issues was The Missionary Position. (This is a very clever joke and a 'play on words'. I'm not quite sure why it is funny but Cherry laughed so much when she thought of it one night when we were trying to make another baby that I told her 'I'd put it in anyway'. When she heard this Cherry said, 'You always do,' and started laughing even harder and got off me and went downstairs to make a cup of camomile and kumquat herbal tea and talk to her friend Carole on the phone.)

So it was easy to know what was The Right Thing To Do.

It wasn't like at Home. That's much more confusing. For instance what is the Moral Position on Foundation Hospitals? Or tax credits and income support? That's why I leave a lot of that stuff to Gordon. He's good at all that and he really likes doing it. That's why it's best that he stays as the Chancellor and that I stay as Prime Minister. In fact when you think about what is Best For The Country it's clear that I have No Choice but to go on being Prime Minister and let him go on running things.

Some Really Important Things That Happened Soon After I Became Prime Minister

A really important thing that happened soon after I became Prime Minister was that I started to get Intelligence Reports. It was just like getting Focus Group reports from Philip With The Glasses except now it was about really important stuff involving National Security.

And it was all Top Secret so I can't really tell you about it.

But one of the scariest Intelligence Reports I got was about Iraq. And Mr Hussein. It was so scary that this is what I said at the time:

'I have now seen some of the stuff on this. It really is pretty scary. He is very close to some appalling Weapons of Mass Destruction.'

And this was in 1997. And shows I was concerned about Iraq and WMD long before George became President and we decided to do a War with Mr Hussein.

Changing Rooms

My first Cabinet Meeting after getting elected was brilliant. It was in a Big Room called The Cabinet Room. And we all sat round a Big Table called The Cabinet Table.

The only problem was that there were so many people. In fact there were too many to really get anything done.

So after that first Cabinet Meeting I went back to my room and got out my diagram of 'The Unfinished Revolution'. I've discovered that it's a really useful drawing to look at when you're not sure what to do.

And the answer was there.

I had Invented New Labour and Saved The Labour Party by having an Inner Core. Then I had won a Landslide Election Victory and Kicked The Tories Out by having an Inner Core. So I had No Choice but to Run The Country and Make Things Better For Everyone by having an Inner Core.

And then I found the Perfect Spot for me and The Inner Core to hang out and Decide Things. It was a cosy office that I started to call The Den.

And I decided that if we really wanted to be The Best Government Ever that we'd make the real decisions in The Den. Then we'd go to The Cabinet Room and tell everyone about it. And then the people there could go and tell the people in the House Of Commons. And then the people there could go and tell The People in the Country.

I loved The Den. And it really worked.

And Then

So that's how I ran The Country for my first Term Of Office. And I ran it very well. And everyone was very happy because at long last The Tories Were Out Of Power.

And we had Cool Britannia. Which everyone loved.

And we had The Millennium Dome. Which was a Big Success.

And we had The Mr Ecclestone Affair. Which I solved when I went on telly saying I would never do 'anything improper. I never have. I think most people who have dealt with me think I am a pretty straight sort of guy.'

I did my best Straight Sort Of Guy Look. And everyone realised that they did trust me. So it was all OK.

And that's why they voted for me at the next Election.

So I was all set to do even more running the country and sorting things. And then.

And Then Terrorists Flew Two Jets Into The World Trade Center And Murdered Thousands Of Innocent People

And After That

And after that the world would never be the same.

George had not been President for very long, so he had not had to deal with an International Crisis before. I was very worried that he would Over-react. And Lash Out.

Everyone was very scared. And everyone did not know what to do. And I realised that if I did not work very hard at being an International Leader and World Statesman it could all go horribly wrong.

So I pledged George My Unfailing Support in public. And gave him Full And Frank advice in private. And I asked for my best spies to produce their best Top Secret dossier on who was to blame.

And who was to blame was Mr Bin Laden who was the leader of The al-Qaeda who lived in Afghanistan and were being protected by The Taliban.

So I explained all this to George and I sent him the Top Secret dossier and said we should publish it so people can see who is to blame and then they will understand why we have to invade Afghanistan and get rid of The Taliban.

And George said, 'OK then.'

And then George's friend Don said why don't we get Iraq as well? He said that because he saw it as being a great way to make real a New World Order that him and some other of George's friends had been thinking about for ages. They called it The Project For The New American Century.

And I said, 'No, George, let's not confuse the issue. Iraq is not an issue for now.'

And George said, 'OK then.'

And while all this had been going on I had been talking to lots and lots and lots of other Heads Of State And Government explaining what was happening and why we were doing the right thing. And they all said, 'OK then.'

So after a while I did a Speech about it to the Labour Party Conference.

Here is some of what I said:

The Kaleidoscope Has Been Shaken

In retrospect, the Millennium marked only a moment in time. It was the events of September 11 that marked a turning point in history.

and

This is an extraordinary moment for progressive politics. Our values are the right ones for this age: the power of community, solidarity, the collective ability to further the individual's interests.

and

But values aren't enough. The mantle of leadership comes at a price.

and

So I believe this is a fight for freedom. And I want to make it a fight for justice too. Justice not only to punish the guilty. But justice to bring those same values of democracy and freedom to people around the world.

and

The starving, the wretched, the dispossessed, the ignorant, those living in want and squalor from the deserts of Northern Africa to the slums of Gaza, to the mountain ranges of Afghanistan: they too are our cause.

and

This is a moment to seize. The kaleidoscope has been shaken. The pieces are in flux. Soon they will settle again. Before they do, let us re-order the world around us.

When Alastair read all this again he smiled to himself. So I said, 'Alastair, why are you smiling? This is all very serious stuff.'

And he said, 'I was just thinking that it's a hell of a career arc.'

And I said, 'What do you mean?'

And he said, 'From Trendy Vicar to Messiah.'

But I didn't know what he meant.

And then he said, 'And I was also thinking about Jo Moore.'

And I said, 'That woman. What about her?'

And he said, 'Well, after September 11 the Americans saw an opportunity to reorganise the world around them. And you saw an opportunity to reorganise the world into a new International Community. And all she wanted to do was bury bad news.'

And I said, 'So?'

And he said, 'Well, then maybe her real mistake was that she thought too small.'

But that didn't make any sense at all to me so I explained to Alastair what her real mistake actually was.

But I don't think he was listening.

An Extraordinary Time

Anyway it was an Extraordinary Time. And because something so horrible had happened everyone Pulled Together. And the International Community united with a common purpose. And when I looked at it all I thought this is just how the world should always be.

So me and George and some others did a War on The Taliban who had been giving The al-Qaeda House Room for far too long.

Luckily The Taliban weren't just giving The al-Qaeda House Room but they were also cruel and nasty to their own people. But what really convinced lots of people in the world just how cruel and nasty The Taliban were was when they destroyed two very ancient and very sacred and very big statues. Of Buddha.

We defeated the Dangerous and Uncontrollable Rogue State of Afghanistan and its Evil Taliban masters by doing Bombing Them Back To The Middle Ages.

As it turned out this was quite an easy thing to do.

Alastair said that it was actually 'Quite a step forward for them'. But I didn't know what he meant.

'Fight! Fight! Fight!'

And then George did something very clever. Alastair says The Others must have put him up to it but I think it was George's idea too. Or maybe it was like when I have an idea but don't realise I've had the idea until someone else tells me what the idea is.

(This often happens when you are The Leader Of Your Country because you are so busy running things that you don't have the time to have all your own ideas yourself. That's why I'm thinking of having An Ideas Tsar to be in charge of Ideas and sort it all out.*)

What George did that was very clever was that he Declared War.

---

* 'Tsars' were one of my best ideas. I know this because soon after Getting Into Power I decided that we needed a Drugs Tsar so we got one and that's why there is No Problem With Drugs In Britain Today.

The War On Terrorism

The War that George declared was On Terrorism.

And he said, 'Everybody must decide. You're either with us or you're with the terrorists.'

And this was very clever because no one wanted to be with the terrorists. So everybody had to be with George.

And the other good thing about declaring a War On Terrorism is that you can make War Time Speeches about everyone pulling together (like in the Blitz), and making hard decisions, and bearing heavy costs, and being in it for the long haul, and everyone making sacrifices and how if anyone criticises you then they are being Unpatriotic and Defeatist and are probably The Enemy Within and are On The Side Of The Terrorists.

And what's also clever is that Terrorism is not a country or an evil regime or an evil leader or even an ideology. You can't bomb Terrorism and invade its territory and overthrow its leaders and install a new system. That's because Terrorism is a Concept.

So George had declared war on a Concept. It was a Stroke Of Genius.

The Best Soundbite In The World, Ever!

George's 'War On Terrorism' was The Best Soundbite In The World, Ever! It was a Soundbite that once anyone heard it they could never forget it. And it was a Soundbite that seemed to be so important and so meaningful. But when you thought about it really hard it was a Soundbite that didn't mean anything at all.

It was even better than Kylie's Soundbite in 'Can't Get You Out Of My Head'.

And George's Soundbite had everyone singing all around the world. And if you were a Leader Of Your Country and you weren't singing then you would feel really stupid and out of it. But the best thing about George's Soundbite was that, even if you weren't keen on the whole song, you only had to mouth the words of the Soundbite and everyone would think that you were really joining in.

The Best Thing About The War On Terrorism

But the best thing about the War On Terrorism is that it is a War That Can Never Be Won. And if it can never be won then you never have to stop fighting it.

And that means you can do things that would get you told off in peace time like curbing civil liberties, and making people afraid of foreigners, and making people afraid of Muslims, and increasing surveillance of your own people, and qualifying the right to free speech and spending lots and lots and lots of money on 'Defence'. And when people complain you can look at them with a very stern face and say:

'Hey! Don't you know There's A War On!'

And that would be the end of that.

So that's how we Defeated The Taliban, put The al-Qaeda On The Run, Freed Afghanistan From Tyranny, and began an Endless War.

But at the back of my mind something was still worrying me.

The Thing At The Back Of My Mind That Was Still Worrying Me

The thing at the back of my mind that was still worrying me was Mr Hussein. And his WMD. And now that we were embarked on a War Against Terrorism a truly terrible thought occurred to me. And this was that truly terrible thought:

What if Mr Hussein gave some of his Weapons Of Mass Destruction to The Terrorists?

And he might do this because he was Evil. And so were the Terrorists. So surely it would only be a matter of time before they got together. And I wasn't going to stand by and Let That Happen. No matter how far off in the distance the possibility seemed to be.

Luckily George and his friends were thinking the same thing. And the more George and his friends talked about it the more real the threat became.

And what was even more lucky was that they had wanted to get rid of Mr Hussein for ages. In fact, even when Bill was The President they had passed a law in Congress saying 'Let's get rid of Mr Hussein'. But because this sounded a bit nasty they did a Makeover on it and called it Regime Change.

But Bill had never really wanted to do much about it. And in the end he was too busy doing cigar sex with Monica With The Stains. And then saying he didn't do sex with Monica With The Stains. And then saying he didn't do sex with Monica With The Stains but that he did do oral sex with her which isn't really sex.

And the funny thing about all this is that Monica With The Stains wasn't even Bill's wife!* This is called having an Affair.

But because he was having an Affair and dealing with the consequences he didn't really have time to do Regime Change on Mr Hussein.

But me and George didn't have Affairs. We were each Very Happily Married to both of our wives. So we weren't

---

*Bill's wife was called Hillary and she did not have Stains.

too busy to do Regime Change on Mr Hussein.

George's Second Best Soundbite

One of the ways that fighting a War is just like fighting an Election is that you have to Win The Hearts And Minds Of The People. If you don't do that they won't let you do a War.

But what's good is that The People don't like to think too hard about War. This is because War is a Very Serious Matter. And War is scary. That is why it is very, very Important that The People can Trust their Leaders when a War is coming.

They want to be able to look at their Leaders and think, 'Yes, I Trust this Leader. He wouldn't lead my country into a War unless we really needed to do a War and there was No Choice.'

And because I was 'A Straight Sort Of Guy' The People Trusted Me.

And in America they Trusted George. And because in America they were still in Shock after The Twin Towers, and still Angry and Embattled, and still engulfed in the Camaraderie of Conflict, and still wanting to Kick Ass, they were really ready To Be Led.

The man who wrote George's speeches called it a 'plastic, teachable moment'. And he then wrote a great Speech for George. In it George said one sentence on North Korea, one on Iran and five on Iraq. And then he said,

States like these, and their terrorist allies, constitute an Axis Of Evil arming to threaten the peace of the world. By seeking weapons of mass destruction, these regimes pose a grave and growing danger. I will not wait on events while dangers gather.

And what was brilliant was that just by saying Axis Of Evil he had linked together in the minds of The People Iran and Iraq and North Korea and Terrorists and Weapons Of Mass Destruction.

And what was even more brilliant is while there was very little, if any, evidence to link all these things together, just by saying it out loud George made it seem very real. And what was Very Clever is that when George said 'terrorist allies' The People in America heard 'The al-Qaeda'. And The al-Qaeda were the ones who had murdered all the people in The Twin Towers.

So with just one Soundbite in one speech made on Tuesday the twenty-ninth of January, only four months after September 11, on prime time television watched by 51 million Americans, George had Won The Hearts And Minds Of The People.*

So now they would let him do a War.

This made George very happy because doing a War with Mr Hussein was a family tradition. But his dad didn't

---

*What was also very clever of George is that he had linked Iran and Iraq together as allies even though they were Sworn Enemies. But then again he might just have been Confused. Because when Iran and Iraq and America are in the same room it is very confusing. I wanted to explain it all to you but I couldn't work out how. But then one afternoon Cherry was watching a repeat of *ER* with George Clooney in it and I had a Good Idea. Here is my Good Idea. (Just read this next bit with an American accent and exciting music in the background.)

'Previously in *The Middle East*:
1952: Mr Mossadegh takes power in Iran and declares full national control of oil resources.
1954: Mr Mossadegh Deposed In CIA-Supported Coup. Mr Shah

Finish Mr Hussein Off When He Had The Chance. So now George could do that for him.

---

of Iran becomes Puppet of US who help him set up secret police.

1958: King of Iraq overthrown by Mr al-Quassim. Later Mr al-Quassim Deposed In CIA-Supported Coup that puts Ba'athist Party in power.

1968: Revolt in Iraq puts Mr Bakr in power with Mr Hussein as his Number Two.

1972: Mr Bakr nationalises Iraqi oil so Mr Nixon arms Iraqi Kurds and also arms Iran.

1979: Mr Shah of Iran deposed by Mr Khomeini in "popular nationalistic, fundamentalist, anti-American revolt". Mr Khomeini annoys Mr Carter by taking some Embassy Hostages but the Soviet Union makes friends with him. Mr Hussein takes over Iraq and the Americans think it would be a Good Idea for Mr Hussein to attack Iran.

1980: Mr Hussein attacks Iran for eight years using American arms. Don, who is George's friend now, visits Mr Hussein to Sort Things Out.

1988: Iran–Iraq war ends. Mr Hussein says he's won, but Iraq is broke. US says, 'Sorry, but if we help you any more, you might get too powerful or you might attack Israel.'

1990: Iraq does an invasion of Kuwait so UN passes sanctions and lots of Iraqi children die.

1991: George's Dad and his friends drive Mr Hussein and the Bad Iraqis out of Kuwait and tell the Good Iraqis to get rid of Mr Hussein themselves, but then don't help them so Mr Hussein crushes the revolt.'

I know this is Confusing but I think it dispels another Popular Misconception. The Popular Misconception it dispels is that one of the reasons George did a War on Mr Hussein was because it was Unfinished Business but actually it was Ongoing Business.

My Problem

My problem was that The People in Britain weren't so ready To Be Led.

That is because they Weren't Sure about a lot of things. They Weren't Sure that Mr Hussein had WMD. They Weren't Sure that Mr Hussein was linked to The al-Qaeda. They Weren't Sure that Britain was really threatened. They Weren't Sure that any threat was imminent. And they Weren't Sure that America was doing The Right Thing for The Right Reason.

But I was Sure Enough For Everyone. That is because Being Sure is one of the things I'm best at. So now my job as Leader Of My Country was to make The People as Sure as I was.

But this wouldn't be a problem because one of the other things I'm best at is Convincing People That I Am Right.

Other Reasons Why I Was Right

And I knew I was right about wanting to Do Regime Change on Mr Hussein because WMD and Terrorism weren't the only reasons that he was bad. He was bad because he was Evil and a Dictator who had tortured and killed hundreds of thousands of his own people. And he had even used WMD on his own people.

He had used WMD in 1988 on them at a place called Halabjah. This was during the Iran–Iraq War after the town had been captured by Kurdish rebels who had handed it over to the Iranians. Mr Hussein gassed the town as revenge and 5,000 people including lots of little children were killed.

This was when Mr Hussein was still an Ally Of The West because he was doing War with the Iranians. But The British Government Had To Act so it sent a Firm

And Clear Message to him by condemning his actions in the Harshest Terms and then later doubling the Export Credits it had extended to him. (Just to show there were no hard feelings.)

But all this was before I was Prime Minister and so has Nothing To Do With Me.

And Mr Hussein didn't have Democracy which is Clearly The Best Way To Run A Country.* Anyway to me the issue was Black & White. Mr Hussein was a Bad and Evil man and he had to go. And it was the Duty of the International Community to see that this came about. And because I was My Brother's Keeper and I Wouldn't Walk By On The Other Side I knew that just like over Kosovo and Afghanistan where my Doctrine Of The International Community had been such a success it was my Moral Duty to lead the way.

And what's more Mr Hussein was Constantly Flouting The Will of the UN and so was Undermining The UN. And this was a very bad thing. Because if the UN was Undermined then things would be Very Bad For Everyone. So by taking the Courageous Course of Action that I saw as my Moral Duty I would also be Saving The UN.

---

*But obviously when we do bring Democracy to Iraq it will have to be a different type of Democracy from ours or America's because if they had the same type of Democracy as us the Shias who are in the majority would win and they are quite close to the fundamentalists who run things in Iran and George and his friends wouldn't be too keen on that so it's probably better if we create a Democracy where 'everyone is represented' and so has a Balance Of Power where no one group can become Too Powerful.

What Alastair Said When
I Showed All This To Him

This is what Alastair said when I showed all this to him:

'It's a bit fucking confusing.'

And I said, 'No, Alastair, it's all perfectly clear.'

And he said, 'Well, mate, in your mind maybe, but it doesn't read that way. It reads like you've done a right Roman Abramovich and gone into the transfer market, bought everything in sight and hoped you'll end up with a football team that might, in your dreams, actually win something.'

And I said, 'I don't follow you.'

And Alastair said, 'Well, the problem's not about people following me. It's about people following you. Go on like this and no one will be able to fathom out why they followed you into a fucking war.'

By now I was getting a bit cross with Alastair. After all I was the Prime Minister!

So this is what I said: 'Well, if you're so blooming clever, Mr Spin Consultant, why don't you come up with an idea to make it easier to follow?'

So Alastair thought for a moment and then he said, 'What it needs is some kind of structure. It needs a framework over which you can organise things, otherwise people are just going to get lost.'

And then he said, 'Also I think people need to understand what it was like in the build-up to the War. You know, how exciting it was. How there was so much going on. How it was easy to get carried away by the momentum of it all.'

And I said, 'You mean how much it was like fighting an Election?'

And he said, 'Yes.'

And I thought about all this and I realised that it was Important. So I got out my Letts Prime Minister's Diary and started looking up what I'd written in it every night over the period leading up to the War.

And when Alastair saw this he said, 'That's the answer. You need a diary of events. That way you can explain what happened, why it happened and when it happened. And how intense it all was.'

And I said, 'OK then.'

And Alastair even thought up a great heading for it.

THE TIMETABLE TO WAR

29 January 2002
The Axis Of Evil Speech
George's speech was made up of sixty-three long paragraphs. He spoke for forty-eight minutes which is longer than the whole first half of a football match if there is no injury time. He ended by saying,

> *Steadfast in our purpose, we now press on. We have known freedom's price. We have shown freedom's power. And in this great conflict, my fellow Americans, we will see freedom's victory.*

But like I said earlier, all anyone remembered was The Axis Of Evil.

March 2002
George Says, 'Fuck Saddam. We're Taking Him Out.'
Obviously he said this in private.

So George gets his Top General to look through The Pentagon's existing sixty-seven war plans and find the one on Iraq and revise it. The new plan is called Op Plan 1003. It is a 90-day build-up, 45-day war, 90-day stabilization plan. Its 225 days would have seven lines of operation aimed at nine slices of regime power. And the Top General tells his Army, Navy, Air Force and Marines commanders: 'This is fucking serious. You know, if you guys think this is not going to happen, you're wrong. You need to get off your ass.'

(I think George must have been really busy at this point because he didn't have time to ring me and get me involved in any of this planning and decision making.)

6–7 April 2002
Me And George Meet Up In Texas

George invited me and the family over to his place at Crawford in Texas for the weekend. We all stayed together and had meals round a big table. It was just like *Dallas*. Me and the kids really got into the spirit of things by going round saying 'Yee-ha!' to each other at the end of every sentence. This is an example of what I mean:

Me: 'Pass the salt, please. Yee-ha!'

Marianne: 'Sure thing, Pa. Yee-ha!'

Mick: 'I'll take ma eggs over easy, Ma. Yee-ha!'

Cherry: 'Tony, maybe the pyjamas-and-Stetson look would have been better left in the bedroom.'

Me: 'You didn't say "Yee-ha." Yee- ha!'

Cherry: 'Oh for fuck's sake.'

Then Cherry went off to find a drink with George's daughters. I thought it was great that she was really getting into the Sue Ellen spirit.

The other thing that happened was that me and George talked about doing War on Mr Hussein. He was very keen on doing War. He was so keen that he would have been happy to do War just by himself.

One thing was clear. I had got here just in time.

So I explained to George that while I agreed that we might have to do a War with Mr Hussein what we needed to do was get The International Community on our side (just like we did over Afghanistan) and that we must work on the Middle East Peace Plan and that the best way of doing everything would be through the UN.

George wasn't that keen on all this but when I explained to him just how important it all was and because he respected me as a World Leader he said, 'OK then.'

Once again my ability to persuade people what the

best thing was to do had helped the Americans come to the right decision.

And even though I didn't say it out loud, inside I did a big 'Yee-ha!'

May–August 2002
I Go To Work

When I got back home I soon began getting reports that George's friends Don and Dick were still telling George to Get On With It. So me and my team spent a lot of time on the phone explaining why my Plan was the best and why there was No Choice but to do the Middle East Peace Plan and Building An International Coalition and Working Through The UN.

And I had the 'prudent' idea of putting George and the White House on our Friends And Family list so that we kept the bills down. (See, Gordon, I *had* been listening to you.)

To make sure that George stuck to my plan I did Reassuring Him. And what I Reassured Him was that I was on his side. This was Very Clever because it made it seem to him that I had made A Commitment when I hadn't really!

Anyway I was Sure that I could build an International Coalition. And I was Sure that I could get the UN to agree to what I wanted. I knew it would take Hard Work, but I had never been afraid of Hard Work.

What I Think About The UN

What I think about the UN is that it is Good, but it is Old Fashioned.

In many ways it is just like Fettes College. And in many ways it is just like the old Labour Party. What I mean is that it needs to change because the world has changed. And if I wasn't so busy I would be just the person to change it.

But it is the only truly Global Forum we have so for the moment, until I can come up with something better, it is best that the UN is involved in things.

Also The People in Britain think the UN is a Good Idea. So if I could get the UN to support my plan then it would be so much easier for me to Win The Hearts And Minds of The People in Britain.

What The Americans Think About The UN

What the Americans think about the UN is that it's just a place where people shout at them. And where countries with the same GDP as Des Moines, Iowa can tell them to behave and stop being such a bully.

And they really don't like the fact that the UN Headquarters are in New York so that they have to pretend to be Gracious Hosts to all these people they really would prefer not to have doing a Sleepover.

7 September 2002
At Camp David I Show George My Cojones

When you're a Leader Of Your Country anniversaries are important. That's because The Media love anniversaries. The Media love doing stories that start 'One Year After …' one year after something important has happened.

It's like that line in the John Lennon (who was in The Beatles) 'Happy Christmas' song.

I mention all this because 7 September 2002 was almost one year after 11 September 2001. So everyone was thinking about The Twin Towers a lot. And George would have to talk about it on 11 September. And he had booked in to make a big Speech to the UN the next day.

I thought it best that I go over and see him before he did so that I could remind him of My Plan and make sure that he didn't Say Anything Silly at the UN.

I was going to make sure that he stayed On Message. Just like in an Election.

Because we haven't had a drawing for a while I thought that this would be a good point to think of a drawing that explains how I saw my role with the US.

This is the drawing that I thought of:

In this drawing the US is a Very Big Ship and I am the *only* Plucky Little Tug Boat that can guide it into a safe mooring.

I showed this drawing to Alastair and asked him what kind of Very Big Ship the US should be. And he thought about this for a moment and then said, 'An aircraft carrier.'

But I told him I couldn't draw those.

And then Alastair said, 'What about an oil tanker?' But I didn't know what he meant.

Anyway on September the seventh I went off to see George at Camp David.

Now because I am part of the Rock'N'Roll generation music has always been a very important part of my life. And when I've been writing this book I've realised that at Significant Moments in my life different bits of music seem to sum up what's been going on. That's why I think this book should have a soundtrack. I'm sure it would be a Smash Hit.

The Camp David meeting should definitely have music playing in the background. And the music it should have is the music from *The Good, The Bad And The Ugly*. The whistling music.

When I got there it was me and George. Face to face. And I knew I couldn't blink. George looked me in the eye and said, 'Saddam Hussein is a threat. And we must work together to deal with this threat, and the world will be better off without him.' And he said it might mean War and that I might have to send troops.

So I looked him in the eye and said, 'I'm with you.'

And I said we should go through the UN first but if that doesn't work Britain Will Back You In Doing War With Iraq.

And it was after this when I was out of the room that George looked Alastair in the eye and said, 'Your man has Cojones.'

And later on when Alastair explained to me what Cojones were I had to agree. I did have Cojones. That's because I had given my word that I would lead My Country in doing a War with Mr Hussein whether the UN agreed or not. And I hadn't even got the agreement of The Cabinet. Or of Parliament.

I had made the decision and I had made the commitment to do a War all by myself!

And this was six whole months before we even had the debate in The House Of Commons about whether we should do a War.

So I most definitely had Cojones.

12 September 2002
George Stays On Message

On September the twelfth George made his speech to the UN. It was the twenty-fourth draft of the speech so obviously George and his friends had been arguing a lot about it.

Some drafts said he would go through the UN. Some drafts said he wouldn't.

In the end the speech said: 'We will work with the UN Security Council for the necessary resolutions.'

This had been my idea all along. So George had stayed On Message.

Now all I had to do was get the UN on board and everyone at home too and then when Mr Hussein saw that the International Community was United against him he would either choose to Call It A Day or we would do a War with him and get rid of him and his WMD that way.

Of course I hoped that he would go of his own accord. That's because I didn't want to do a War unless we really had to. But if we had No Choice, then we had No Choice.

But I wasn't that worried about it all because I was Certain Of My Case. And I was certain that I could convince the International Community, even in the old-fashioned UN, that I was right.

So my commitment to George wasn't that much of a risk after all!

13–17 September 2002
WMD – My Best Soundbite

The thing that would most convince the UN to agree that Mr Hussein was a threat was WMD. And what was good was that this was exactly the same thing that would Win The Hearts And Minds Of The People in Britain too.

But this Winning Hearts And Minds was slightly different from Winning Hearts And Minds in an Election. In an Election you have to make the Hopes and the Fears balance.

But in this situation, because The People don't like anything that might lead to War, you have to make the Fears so much bigger than the Hopes.

In fact you have to make them more afraid of what might happen if you don't do a War.

But luckily WMD was the perfect Soundbite for doing just that!

For a start no one really knew what a WMD actually was. But it did sound Very, Very Scary. And because we had such good relations with The Media, and pretended to let them in on what was happening, and WMD made a great headline, when we started talking about WMD to them they all started using it without really asking what it meant!

And even on the plane back from Camp David I had begun to get the Media onside by 'sharing' with them my fear of WMD:

I'm not saying it will happen next month, or even next year, but at some point the danger will explode.

This is not an American preoccupation. It is our pre-occupation. It must be the preoccupation of the entire world.

And because I was doing my best Gravitas look when I 'shared' this with them they knew that I was being Serious.

And by focusing on WMD I realised that I could 'turn something complicated, multi-layered and dynamic into a simple, sustainable communicable truth that influenced people' just like Philip With The Glasses used to say you had to do if you wanted to win an Election.

And I'd never lost an Election yet.

All I needed to do now was to build up the case about WMD.

We Do Another Dossier

What I decided we needed was a Dossier. I decided this because a Dossier had worked in the past. Before we did War on The Taliban in Afghanistan we published a Dossier that showed the link between The Taliban and The al-Qaeda and the attack on The Twin Towers.

That Dossier was clear, and it was precise, and it was detailed. And anyone who read it could be in No Doubt that it justified the International Community in doing War on Afghanistan.

So we needed a Dossier just like that for Iraq and Mr Hussein.

So I told my Top Spies, 'Hey, guys, we need a Dossier just like the Afghanistan one, but for Iraq and Mr Hussein.'

And because we all knew that Mr Hussein had WMD and was also Working To Acquire more WMD we knew that WMD would feature heavily in the Dossier.

Because there wasn't much time my Top Spies had to get their under-spies to work much faster than they were used to. And the under-spies had to get their under-under-spies to work even harder.

Alastair called it 'The Buzzing Around Like A Blue Arsed Spy' period. Which was very funny.

17 September 2002
Mr Scarlett, In The Den, With The Dossier

Mr Scarlett, who was my Top Top Spy, presented the new Dossier to us on the morning of September the seventeenth. I thought it was Very Convincing. But some others didn't. They said it didn't show clearly enough that Mr Hussein was a threat.

Jonathan, who was my Chief of Staff, even said:

The document does nothing to demonstrate a threat, let alone an imminent threat from Saddam. In other words it shows he has the means but does not demonstrate he has the motive to attack his neighbours, let alone the west. We will need to make it clear in launching the document that we do not claim that we have evidence that he is an imminent threat.

But I remained Convinced. But then again I had been Convinced even before we had the Dossier.

A lot of people have said that we 'Sexed Up' the Dossier. But we didn't. All we did was take what was in the Dossier and made sure that it was put across in the most Convincing way possible. Just like we would have done if the Dossier was the script for a Party Political Broadcast during an Election campaign. And what could possibly be wrong with that?

When I showed this bit to Alastair to see if this was how

he remembered it he said it was. And then he said and that's why he had got so 'fucking narked' when the BBC accused him of 'Sexing Up The Dossier'.

And then he laughed.

So I asked him, 'I thought this made you angry, so why are you laughing?'

And he said, 'Typical fucking BBC, always getting the story wrong.'

And I said, 'So why is that funny?'

And he said, 'Well, if they hadn't been so busy going on about "Sexing Up The Dossier" they would have realised the real issue was Sexing Down The Caveats.'

But he never explained what he meant.

24 September 2002
Iraq's Weapons Of Mass Destruction – The Assessment Of The British Government

This is what we called the Dossier. It made it sound very Official. And very Serious. And we made sure all the Media knew just how Serious it all was.

And we published the Dossier on the day the House of Commons was recalled. And I made a Speech about it to the House of Commons.

In the foreword to the Dossier I wrote:

documents show that some of Iraq's WMD could be ready for use within forty-five minutes. *

and

---

*Later on it turned out that this referred only to 'battlefield' WMD! And that the 'intelligence' came from a single uncorroborated source. In fact, my Top Spies got the information from a bloke

Saddam's WMD programme is active, detailed and growing.

It was a Very Convincing Dossier. And I made a Very Convincing Speech.

But even after I made my Convincing Speech and presented the Convincing Dossier some people weren't Convinced which I thought was very curious.

The *Financial Times* said that there was 'No compelling evidence that immediate military action was needed'.

Luckily, though, most of the tabloids were much more sensible. And just like in an Election it was the tabloids that were the most important. So it was clear that we were getting the right message across to the right people.

Some of the other people who were still not convinced were the leaders of the EU countries but I didn't worry too much because I was Sure Of My Case and I had Total Faith in my Powers Of Persuasion.

The Bridge Over Troubled Water
At this point I should probably talk about another way that I see my role and Britain's role in the world. Or better still I can do another drawing.

---

called Abdul one Friday night in Baghdad. Obviously if I had known all this I wouldn't have made such a Big Thing about it. But when you're the Leader of Your Country you're often too busy to consider all the unimportant details of the things you talk about. Especially if you're Very Busy trying to Win The Hearts And Minds Of The People in case you have to lead them into a War.

Later still it turned out that Mr Hussein didn't even have 'battlefield' WMD because he didn't use them when there was a battlefield.

This is the drawing.

It is a Bridge.

And that is how I think of myself. And of Britain. In the New World Order that is emerging in the new Millennium we are a Bridge. On one side of the Bridge is The United States and on the other side of the Bridge is Europe. And we are what links the two sides together.

I think it is a Vital Role. And being the Bridge would never be more vital than now when The Americans and The Europeans seemed to be getting further and further apart.

When I showed this to Alastair this is what he said:

'A bridge for the new Millennium?'

And I said, 'Yes.'

And he said, 'That makes you The Millennium Bridge.'

And I said, 'Yes. That's exactly what I am.'

And he said, 'Are you sure that's an image you want to put in people's minds?'

But I don't know why he said that.

25 September–8 November 2002
All Aboard The 1441 To Baghdad Central

What I needed now was to get the Security Council of the UN to pass a Resolution that would either convince Mr Hussein to get rid of his WMD, or if he didn't get rid of them then it would say it was all right for us to do a War with him.

This would be Very Tricky because some of the other countries on the Security Council of the UN didn't think it was that urgent that we do War with Mr Hussein.

The other problem was that even though George had said that he would go through the UN lots of his friends didn't think it was a Good Idea so were determined to make it fail.

They tried to make it fail by making the Resolution as Hard Line as possible. They wanted either for the other members of the Security Council to turn it down as being too harsh or for Mr Hussein to Refuse To Comply for the same reason.

I thought this Wasn't Really Playing The Game.

Later on I discovered that the other reason they wanted the UN route to fail is that they had already decided that the best time to do a War with Mr Hussein would be in the Spring of 2003.

The main reasons why they didn't want to wait too long before doing a War were that:

1 They didn't want to do a War in the summer when it would be too hot.
2 They didn't want their troops to have to sit round too long in position and get bored.
3 They didn't want uncertainty over a War to affect their economy.
4 They didn't want the War to spill over into 2004 when there would be an Election for President.

And the funny thing is that none of these reasons had anything to do with Mr Hussein or what he was doing or even his WMD.

So I had to work very hard to come up with a Resolution that the Security Council would agree with. The main person who helped me was Jack who was my Foreign Secretary. Jack wasn't Foreign and he wasn't my Secretary, but he was in charge of chatting with other countries. To get the Resolution through he had to do a lot of chatting.

And in America I found that Co-Lin, who is confusingly spelt Colin, was also very keen on getting the UN to agree and getting the UN to disarm Mr Hussein. Co-Lin was the Top Black Person In America and The Top Soldier too.

Surprisingly despite being The Top Soldier he was much less keen on doing War then a lot of George's friends like Don and Dick. But maybe this was because he Really Knew What War Was Like.

I told Jack that to Get On The Same Wavelength as Co-Lin he should use these phrases:

'Yo, Homey Numba One! Wassup?'

'Respec'!'

'You Da Man!'

Which must have worked because they got on really well.

And in the end we got Everyone on the Security Council to agree to Resolution 1441.

Everyone Should Have A Wiggle Room
This is the Really Clever Bit. We got everyone to agree to Resolution 1441 by building into it Wiggle Room. Since I've been Running The Country I've discovered just how important Wiggle Room is.

Wiggle Room is when you're coming up with the words that say what you're going to do, you make them Sound Very Precise, but you leave enough room in the gaps between the words so that later on you can Wiggle about and end up doing pretty much whatever you want.

In Resolution 1441 the Wiggle Room mainly was about what exactly Mr Hussein would have to do to break the agreement about Disarming. Also who would decide whether he had broken the agreement. And what the 'Serious Consequences' that would result actually meant. And whether we had to go back to the Security Council and get them to say 'Yes you can do a War' before we did a War.

And because we'd built in so much Wiggle Room everyone on the Security Council agreed because everyone could interpret it pretty much how they wanted to.

So Resolution 1441 was passed unanimously.

But what not many people know is that I Really Do Have A Real Wiggle Room. It's in the basement in Downing Street. It's a copy of the discotheque in *Saturday Night Fever* and after a hard day Running The Country I put on a white suit, and Let Off Steam by having a good Wiggle.

These are some of Favourite Songs To Wiggle To:

'When Will I Be Famous?' by Bros
'Rebel, Rebel' by David Bowie
'Born To Run' by Bruce 'The Boss' Springsteen
'Things Can Only Get Better' by D:ream
'I'd Like To Teach The World To Sing' by The New
    Seekers
'War' by Edwin Starr
'I Will Survive' by Gloria Gaynor

I'm also quite keen on anything by Busted.

Why The Americans Really Agreed To Resolution 1441

This shows just how hard it is to spot what is Really Going On in the Diplomatic Language of a UN Resolution. And how confusing it can all be. Even to the experts.

In order to agree to the other bits of the Resolution which seemed Much More Important, George and his friends got another clause put into the Resolution saying that Mr Hussein had to make a Full Declaration of all his WMD and WMD plans.

This didn't sound like such a Big Deal. So The Others (who were the French and the Russians) on the Security Council said, 'Oh, all right then.' But what they hadn't spotted was that this new clause was a Cunning Trap.

That's because the Americans thought that if Mr Hussein said in his Full Declaration that he had WMD, then he would have been violating existing UN Resolutions so they could do a War with him. And if Mr Hussein said in his Full Declaration that he didn't have WMD, then he would be lying to the UN and so they could do a War with him again.

Which shows just how Sneaky the Americans can be.

9 November–6 December 2002
Mr Hussein Does Something Clever

Then what happened is that Mr Hussein read the Resolution. And he Thought About It. And he Did Something Clever.

He invited the Weapons Inspectors back. And he said they could go wherever they wanted. And talk to whoever they wanted.

This was Clever because while everyone else thought Weapons Inspectors were a Good Thing, the Americans didn't. They thought Weapons Inspectors were a waste of time. And when they heard that the Top Weapons Inspector would be Mr Blix they were even more convinced. That's because Mr Blix was Foreign and was bound not to look Very Hard for WMD.

And the Americans had never been very keen on Weapons Inspectors. Even back in 1998 when the Weapons Inspectors had verifiably got rid of 90–95 per cent of Iraq's WMD capability. And back then the Americans even had CIA spies working for them in the UN Weapons Inspection teams.

But because they didn't think that the Weapons Inspections were working they made up a crisis over inspecting Presidential Palaces that led to the Inspectors being withdrawn.

When Alastair read this he said, 'Are you sure they didn't make up the crisis not because the weapons inspections weren't working, but because they were?'

There is a word for this kind of thinking. The word is 'Cynical' and I have always been against it. I told Alastair this and he smiled but I don't know why.

So the Americans didn't want the Weapons Inspectors to go back in. They thought it was just Mr Hussein Playing For Time. But the Weapons Inspectors went back in. And the Americans Weren't Happy.

7 December 2002
Much Longer Than Harry Potter

On December the seventh Mr Hussein sent over to the UN a Full Declaration all about his Weapons and Weapons Programmes. It was 11,807 pages long. This was much longer than *all* the Harry Potter stories put together.

But when the Americans read it they said it was just a warmed-up rehash of what he'd written about WMD years before. But then again he'd only had 30 days to write it in.

And there were the weekends to take into account. And maybe some people were away on holiday.

Anyway the Americans Weren't Happy.

And when I saw how Unhappy they were I decided Not To Be Happy Too.

So this is what I told the guys in The Den: 'This was his big opportunity. He's blown it.'

18 December 2002
George Gets A Bit Confused

During all this time I wasn't the only one trying to get the International Community all together. George was doing it too. On Wednesday the eighteenth of December he had a meeting with José (who used to be the Spanish Leader) in the Oval Office.

It was a Good Meeting because José already wanted to do a War.

George said, 'The declaration is nothing, it's empty, it's a joke.'

And he said, 'If the decision is made to go to war, we'll go back to the Security Council. We won't ask for permission, we will ask for support. That was the agreement with Security Council members. Security Council won't have a veto.'

This just shows how easy it is to get Confused about the UN because even someone in such an important position as President of the United States didn't really understand what had been agreed. And he didn't realise that the five permanent members of the Security Council always have a veto. Which is surprising because the Americans had used their Veto loads of times in the past.

And then George said, 'War is my last choice. Saddam Hussein is using his money to train and equip al-Qaeda with chemicals, he's harbouring terrorists.'

And this just shows how someone as Clever as the President of the United States can get a bit confused about other things too because there was no real evidence linking Mr Hussein to The al-Qaeda. In fact, Mr Hussein and Mr Bin Laden probably wouldn't be friends at all because Mr Hussein was No Respecter Of Religion and his regime had suppressed the Shia Muslim majority and didn't let them practise their faith and had killed hundreds of Muslim clerics.

And the funny thing is that George could get a bit confused even though he was The Most Powerful Man In The World, with the Largest Intelligence Network That Ever Existed at his beck and call. And he was even Commander In Chief Of The Mightiest War Machine The World Has Ever Seen.

Christmas 2002
Nothing Decent On The Telly

Over Christmas there was nothing decent on the telly. And when there was something interesting about What Was Going On In The World it was always about how unconvinced a lot of the public still were. And how unconvinced a lot of the New Labour Party still were.

And even in The Cabinet there were people who were unconvinced. The most unconvinced person in the Cabinet was Robin. And he kept asking the same questions: 'Why War?' and 'Why Now?'

That's when I sadly had to come to the conclusion that Robin might well be The Enemy Within. But then again I was starting to think that about the French. And maybe even also about Mr Blix and his Weapons Inspectors in Iraq.

Anyway because there was nothing decent on the telly I thought I'd do a bit of reading about Iraq.

What I Discovered About Iraq

What I discovered about Iraq is that it was an ancient and historic place because it was the birthplace of civilisation. It is where Mesopotamia flourished. Where writing was invented. And where cities are still occupied that date back to 5000 BC.

I also discovered that the British had invented Iraq.

That was in 1917 when what was still called Mesopotamia was part of the Turkish Ottoman Empire which the British defeated in the First World War.

We then did a secret deal with The French, who were our Allies back then,* which drew up the borders of 'Iraq' and also let us stay in charge.

The Iraqis Revolted against us in 1920 but we crushed them by doing the First Systematic Aerial Bombardment In History. Mr Churchill thought it might be a Good Idea for the RAF to use Poison Gas against the rebelling Kurds.

When I read this I thought that the poor Kurds must be getting Sick And Tired of poison gas being used against them. And I also thought it sounded just like one of the Biggles books I used to read at school. It could have been called *Biggles And The Poison Gas*.

Then in 1921 we put King Faisal on the throne. Then in 1932 we let Iraq become an 'independent' nation. But the King was still Our Man. In the 1930s there were lots of coups. And by 1941 a pro-Nazi, anti-British regime was in power. So we landed a force at Basra and occupied the country again. For the next seventeen years the country was run by Mr Said who was a Good Friend of the British.

Then in 1958 there was another coup and both King

---

*This is what is called 'ironic'.

Faisal II and Mr Said were murdered. And that's when we decided it was probably time to get out.

It all sounded Very Exciting.

But in lots of ways I Disapproved Of It All. That is because it all sounded like an Exercise of Colonial Power. And it had very little to do with us being involved in Iraq now. Because now we were getting involved in order to secure a Safer World. And to Free The People of Iraq. And to bring them Democracy.

And because I am such a 'Straight Sort Of Guy' I was sure that everyone in The Region would see that my motives were Honourable despite everything Britain had got up to in The Past.

While I was doing all this reading Our Forces were building up in the region but I was careful to reassure The People at home this was just to make the Threat Of Military Action seem Credible.

And all the time the Americans were building up their Forces too. And they had a lot of Forces.

January 2003
What I Thought Resolution 1441 Meant

I thought Resolution 1441 meant that we had been Authorised To Use Force. And I was Convinced of this. And the more I talked about it the more Convinced I became.

But a lot of The People in the country weren't Convinced that using Force was the only solution. And neither were a lot of people in the New Labour Party. And neither were a lot of people in The House Of Commons.

But there was one thing that would Convince them.

A Second Resolution from The United Nations Security Council. If a Second Resolution said that we could use Force then everything would be OK.

The Soundtrack Changes

The soundtrack didn't actually change but if this was a film it would. And we would start hearing the music to *Mission Impossible*.

And I would be Tom Cruise. Only taller.

The Inner Core Had Changed

One of the interesting things I realised as I looked around is that The Inner Core had changed. Gordon wasn't involved because this was a Foreign Policy matter so was nothing to do with him. And Peter wasn't around because he'd been a bit silly so I'd had to pretend to Let Him Go.

In many ways it was Only Me In Charge.

But this doesn't mean that other people weren't involved. For example there was The Cabinet but like I've said before The Cabinet had too many people in it to be good at making decisions.

Then there was The War Cabinet, which was like The Cabinet only smaller and met on Thursday mornings just before The Cabinet met.

But when I worked with The War Cabinet I soon discovered that they were 'too formal' and 'insignificantly focused'.

So I cunningly started having informal War Council meetings in The Den before each War Cabinet meeting. The War Council was like The War Cabinet only smaller. In it I only allowed my Top Personal Advisers and the Top Civil Servants who were in charge of spying, defence and foreign chatting. What was good was that none of them was elected so despite all the debates and differing viewpoints they would put it was still Only Me who would have to Make The Decisions.

And it was all really exciting and a bit like Secret Squirrel so we didn't have an agenda or take notes. And to make sure no one knew about this secret War Council In The Den everyone would play a trick and sneak through Number 10 to join the regular War Cabinet meetings as if they'd only just got there!

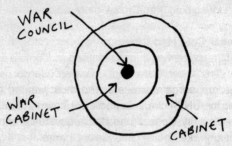

And, of course, I was also having smaller informal meetings all the time with Alastair and Jack and Geoff (who was Defence Secretary but not really that involved in it all) and lots of other people.

So I was really the only one who knew everything that was going on. And so I was the only one who could really Make All The Decisions.

That's why when The Cabinet started to Get Wobbly about it all and how Badly Things Seemed To Be Going I could do my best Reassuring Face and say:

'Trust me. I know my way through this.'

And the way through it was to get a Second Resolution.

So I got all my Top Diplomats and said that we had to win support for this and that we had to really Go For It. I said they had to turn the volume knob on the Diplomacy speakers Up To Eleven. But they didn't know what I meant. Obviously none of them had ever seen This Is Spinal Tap.

20 January 2003
The French Ambush Co-Lin
This was very mean. Co-Lin had gone to the UN for a meeting about Terrorism. But the French Foreign Minister really had a go at him about America's preparation for War. And what was worse was that in a press conference afterwards the French Foreign Minister said 'Nothing! Nothing!' justified war.

This got Co-Lin really angry. That's because he was the one of George's advisers who most wanted to go through the UN Security Council. But now a member of the UN Security Council had had a go at *him* and had made it look like The Security Council were Just Kidding when they talked about 'Serious Consequences' for Mr Hussein if he didn't Disarm.

20 January 2003 as well
'Who Do You Think You Are Kidding, Mr Hussein?'
To show Mr Hussein (and everyone else) that we weren't Just Kidding I told Geoff to tell Parliament that we were committing 35,000 troops (a quarter of the British army) and 100 aircraft (a third of the RAF's front-line force) to the region.

21 January 2003
What George Said To Show He Meant Business
This is what George said to show that he meant business:

I believe in the name of peace, he must disarm. And we will lead a coalition of willing nations to disarm him. Make no mistake about that, he will be disarmed.

The more I looked at what he said, the cleverer I

thought it was. That's because it had two really Good Ideas in it.

The first Good Idea was that we would Fight A War In Order To Have Peace. Which, when you think about it, was just like one of the *Monty Python* sketches I used to think were so funny when I was at Uni. And the funnier thing is that I believed it too!

The second Good Idea was about how the Americans wanted International Relations to operate in their New World Order. This was the Idea:

The Coalition won't define the Mission,
the Mission will define the Coalition.

And it explained how the Americans were going to Run The World.

22 January 2003
What Jacques Said To Show He Was Profound
Jacques was the French Prime Minister. And this is what he said the next day:
'War is always an admission of defeat.'

22 January 2003 as well
What George's Friend Don Said To Show He Could Be Profound Too
This is what George's friend Don said to show he could be profound too:
'You're thinking of Europe as Germany and France. I don't. That's old Europe. If you look at the entire NATO Europe today, the centre of gravity is shifting to the east.'

As for me, I was still busy on the Phone. And busy telling everyone to Trust Me. And busy reassuring everyone that I had things Under Control.

27 January 2003
Mr Blix's First Report
Mr Blix's First Report to the UN Security Council was a real surprise.

Me and George had thought that he wasn't going to be too nasty to Mr Hussein but actually he was. He said Mr Hussein had Not Accepted the need to Disarm and that his Inspectors had been harassed inside Iraq.

This was going to be Very Helpful in my campaign to get a Second UN Resolution. And I was sure it would help me bring Jacques round too.

29 January 2003
George Talks Tough (Again)
Then George had to do a State of the Union Address. This is when he addresses the Union about its State. Everyone watches and everyone knows it is Important.

I think this is a Good Thing To Do. I wish I could do State of the Union Addresses in the United Kingdom. That way I'd be able to tell everyone What's Been Going On and how well I'd been Running Things.

George took a different tack. His tack was called Ass Kicking.

He said he didn't need further UN authorisation. And then he said:

We will consult. But let there be no misunderstanding. If Saddam Hussein does not fully disarm, for the safety of our people and for the peace of the world, we will lead a coalition to disarm him. The course of this nation does not depend upon the decision of others.

Alastair explained it like this. He said George was

saying it's his football so he's going to decide when the game starts.

My problem was that I really had to get More Players on Our Side before it all kicked off.

There was only one thing to do: go to see George.

31 January 2003
I Go To See George

I was supposed to see George at Camp David. But there was too much fog so we met in The White House. There may have been fog outside, but I didn't want The Fog Of War on the inside.*

I Laid It On The Line for George. I said that we needed a Second Resolution.

And George said, 'No we don't.' And so did Dick and Don and even Co-Lin.

I could see that this was going to be Tricky. I racked my brain trying to come up with the precise argument, both logical and moral, that would convince George just why a Second Resolution was so Vitally Important For The World. And then I came up with the answer. And this is what I said:

'George, *I* need a Second Resolution.'

And I explained that I had all but promised one to My Party. And that The People back at home expected one. And if I didn't get one it would be Very Difficult For Me.

And when I explained it to him like that, George agreed and said:

'If that's what you need, we will go flat out† to try and help you get it.'

---

*This is called 'a clever play on words'.

†This turned out to be another 'euphemism'.

He agreed as a Personal Favour to me. And to think some people still think that Britain gets nothing out of being so Supportive of our American Allies!

5 February 2003
Co-Lin Makes the Big Pitch

In order to win the UN over Co-Lin made a Detailed and Convincing presentation to the Security Council about Mr Hussein's WMD.

It took seventy-six minutes which is nearly as long as two halves of a rugger match. It had slides and diagrams and satellite photographs and transcripts of conversations and recordings of conversations. The best bit it had was a teaspoon of simulated anthrax for Co-Lin to wave around in a vial.

It sounded fantastic. And Co-Lin was only saying what I had been saying all along. Surely no one could remain Unconvinced after this!

10 February 2003
The Russians, The Germans And The French Remain Unconvinced

Jacques, Vladimir and Gerhardt formed the 'Non-Nyet-Nein Alliance'. Jacques acted as the main spokesman. This is what he spoke:

> *Nothing today justifies war. Russia, Germany and France are determined to ensure that everything possible is done to disarm Iraq peacefully.*

I asked Alastair what he made of it all. He just looked at me and said, 'Quelle fucking surprise.'
But I didn't know what he meant.
Quite soon after that I began to Hear Rumours that

the real reasons why the French and the Russians didn't want to do a War with Mr Hussein was because of their Extensive Business Links To The Country.

Alastair said that he had Heard Rumours too and that he had No Idea where they came from but if they were true they would Explain A Lot.

Anyway I decided that they weren't the only ones who could play Hard Ball.

I started going on telly to face hostile audiences. And started reporting to Parliament more frequently. Alastair called it my Masochism Strategy.

But I just saw it as the best way of using my Great Powers of Persuasion and tapping into the Great Reservoir Of Trust that The People had built up in me.

14 February 2003
Mr Blix's Second Report
Mr Blix's Second Report said that the Iraqis were co-operating.

And that 400 visits had covered 300 sites.

And that all inspections were at No Notice.

And that they'd looked at industrial sites, ammunition depots, research centres, universities, presidential sites, mobile laboratories, private houses, missile production facilities, military camps and agricultural sites.

And that more than 200 chemical and 100 biological samples had been taken.

And that so far 75 per cent of the samples had been screened and No Prohibited Weapons Or Substances had been found.

There was Only One possible conclusion: Sneaky Mr Hussein was hiding his WMD really well.

I also got a lovely Valentine's Day card. I'm pretty sure that it was from Cherry. But Alastair said it might be from George. But I didn't know what he meant.

15 February 2003
A Bit Of A March In London
There was a bit of a March in London. Some say well over A Million People took part from all over the country and from all Walks of Life. Unfortunately I was up in Glasgow which is north of The North preparing to speak to the New Labour Spring Conference. Otherwise I would have asked to speak at the demonstration and I would have Won Over the protesters to My Point Of View.

But even though the scale of the protest was Impressive it was still a Waste Of Time because they were all wrong and I was right.

What *did* upset me was that some of the demonstrators were suggesting that I was acting immorally. Obviously this wasn't true because I was The Most Moral Person I Knew!

But I didn't get Angry about it, I just got Even More Determined.

The US Embassy in London were rattled by the demonstration. They started to think that I might be in Real Trouble. Of course I wasn't but if I let the Americans think that I was then maybe George would firm up on going after a Second Resolution.

And then we'd get the Second Resolution and then everyone would be happy and everything would be OK.

24 February 2003
George Firms Up On Going After A Second Resolution
Which was nice. For the first time he publicly stated that the US would pursue a Second Resolution. But in private he set a Deadline. The Deadline was mid-March.

The *Mission Impossible* music was getting louder.

And all the time we were doing all the things we had done to win Elections. We were doing Winning Hearts And Minds and Spin and Rapid Rebuttal and Media Monitoring and Staying On Message and Undermining The Enemy Within and Focus Groups and Being Dynamic and Thou Shalt Not Lose and while we didn't actually have a War Room as this would sound Bad we had a War Room Mentality.

And anyway because I couldn't really be sure who was on my side even among the people who should have been on my side a War Room would have been far too big. We needed something smaller. Something only the size of a Bunker.

27 February 2003
'They Smile In Your Face ...'

One hundred and twenty-one of my own New Labour MPs rebelled against the Government and backed a motion that said that the case for War was not proven. It was the largest revolt against Government by its own party members for over 100 years.

But they only did it because I hadn't had the chance to explain things to them in person so they didn't Appreciate The Implications.

And anyway I was rather busy trying to get the Second Resolution sorted out which I thought I could do because on the Security Council as well as the Permanent Members there were always Guest Members too (at this time there were Spain, Mexico, Chile, Bulgaria, Angola, Cameroon and Guinea). If I could get enough of them on my side then we would be OK.

Of the Permanent Members China wasn't that interested and Vladimir could probably be talked round by

George. So the French seemed like the problem. But the French were always Like That and in the end they always Come Round.

Meanwhile in Washington more people were coming over to our side all the time.

5 March 2003
With God On Our Side
Pope John Paul II sent a personal envoy to Washington to meet George and argue against War. The envoy said that there would be civilian casualties. And that it would deepen the gulf between the Christian World and the Muslim World. And that it would not be A Just War. And that it would be illegal. And that it would not make things better.

'Absolutely,' said George, 'it will make things better.'

And I agreed with George.

7 March 2003
Mr Blix's Third Report
This just shows how sneaky Sneaky Mr Hussein can be. That's because he had started co-operating. And even destroying missiles.

Mr Blix said it was:

A substantial measure of disarmament – indeed the first since the mid-1990s. We are not watching the breaking of toothpicks. Lethal weapons are being destroyed.

And he also said that:

the numerous initiatives, which are now taken by the Iraqi side with a view to resolving some long-

standing open disarmament issues, can be seen as
'active' or even 'proactive'.

Mr Blix asked for more time to carry on the work which was at long last really Getting Somewhere.

But the Americans, who never liked Weapons Inspectors or Mr Blix, thought that Mr Hussein was just Stringing Them Along. And I was With The Americans.

7 March 2003 as well
We Table A Resolution

It was Cards On The Table time. Jack put forward a Resolution giving Mr Hussein Ten Days to Come Into Line. If he didn't do this, and no one on the Security Council Vetoed the Resolution, then we would be cleared to do a War.

And now the diplomacy got Turned Up To Twelve and I made lots and lots and lots of phone calls. I was trying to get the Guest Members of the Security Council to at last see sense and realise that I had been right all along.

But the problem was that lots of The People in lots of these countries were Against The War. So their Leaders weren't so keen to join us no matter How Right It Was.

And, to be honest, the Americans weren't trying very hard to win anyone over. But I suppose it was because they were Very Busy Preparing For War.

9 March 2003
George Rings Up

But even though George must obviously have been Very Busy Preparing For War he still made time to call me. And on a Sunday as well.

He said he was very worried that my 'Government Might Go Down'.

And then he said that he'd let us Drop Out of the

coalition and that we could be part of the second wave, as peace keepers perhaps, and that he'd rather go alone than have my government fall which I thought was very nice of him.

And I said, 'I said I'm with you. I mean it. I'm there to the very end.'

I think of this as 'Cojones II'.

10 March 2003
Cojones III – This Time It's Women

To show that I'm Not Afraid to face up to the Harsh Consequences and Brutal Realities of War I put myself In The Line Of Fire with a group of Hostile Women in a television studio interview with Trevor McDonald.

Some of the Women lost sons in the last Gulf War, some had husbands in the army in Kuwait and one was a girl from Australia who lost her boyfriend in the Bali bombing. When I got there they were all Very Angry.

And in many ways the broadcast didn't go well. But everyone could see just how Sincere I was about it all so that was bound to Impress The People.

Trevor McDonald is famous for his 'And finally's'.

The 'And finally' on this interview happened as the credits rolled and some of the women begin to slow handclap me but I don't think that bit got broadcast.

10 March 2003 as well
'Voulez-Vous Couchez Avec Moi – Ce Soir?'

This is another of my Favourite Songs to wiggle to down in The Wiggle Room after a hard day Running Things. But I only wiggle to it when I'm there with Cherry. And we always sing the words to each other.

My favourite bit is the 'ce soir' bit. 'Ce soir' means 'this evening'. And I like it because if you left it out of the song, while the thrust of the song would be much the same, the urgency wouldn't.

In fact, without '*ce soir*' you could argue that the whole tone of the song and even its very meaning would be very different.

What Jacques Said On TV About The New Resolution On The Table

First Jacques said that the French were against it as currently drafted. Then he said that I wouldn't get enough votes for a majority anyway, so he wouldn't have to use the Veto. And then he said,

> *My position is that, regardless of the circum-*
> *stances, France will vote no because it considers*
> *this evening there are no grounds for waging war*
> *in order to achieve the goal we have set ourselves*
> *– to disarm Iraq.*

In many ways this was The End Of Our Diplomatic Efforts. Because if the French were going to vote No, and even use their Veto, then why should the other members on the Security Council risk unpopularity at home by voting with us?

But in other ways it was a Good Thing because now we could Blame The French for the Breakdown In Diplomacy.

So I got Jack to do this at every possible opportunity and I got him to keep repeating that the French had said '… regardless of circumstances, France will vote no …'

And I made sure that Jack left out the rest of what Jacques had said. And especially the '*ce soir*' bit.

And Alastair made sure that the tabloids Got The Message.

12 March 2003
It Ain't Over Till It's Over
George rang up and said, 'It's over.'

13 March 2003
The Seat Of Power
Most of My Important Meetings took place on the sofa in The Den now.

And the great thing about the sofa is that only three of you can fit on it at a time. And you all have to face the same way.

Most of the time it was just me, Alastair and Jack.

14 March 2003
A Lot Of People Are Running Everywhere
Every time I stuck my head out of The Den there were a lot of people running everywhere.

It was quieter in The Den. I could think in there about The Big Battle that was coming. The Big Battle on which So Much Hung.

In four days' time there would be a Debate in The House Of Commons about the War. And after the Debate there would be a Vote.

So I had to win that Vote.

15 March 2003
The War Is Legal!
It was a Saturday but I still went into work and I had a meeting with all my Top New Labour Party people. We discussed Strategy and Tactics on how to win the Vote on Tuesday.

We said, 'This could get Ugly.' And, 'This could get Messy.' But this was War.

As for the actual War we had the Good News that

the Attorney General had decided that War against Iraq would be legal on the basis of past UN Resolutions so it was just like I had always said: we didn't actually need a Second Resolution after all!

But the really Good News was that we'd never have to explain in public the details of the Attorney General's decision on the legality of the War because it just wasn't The Done Thing.

16 March 2003
The Whips Get Whipping And I Go To The Azores

Whipping sounds quite mean and nasty and a bit rude. In fact it sounds a bit like Fagging which I had to go through way back in my days at Fettes College. But it is nothing like that.

Fagging was all about Bullying Prefects getting you to do things that you didn't want to. Whipping is about Senior and Respected members of your party getting other slightly reluctant and easily confused members of your party to do what they really, deep down, want to do because it is The Party Line after all.

Anyway the Whips were Hard At It. They were making sure that everyone in The Party came to the Right Conclusion about things.

And I went to The Azores, in the Atlantic Sea, which is part of Portugal, to meet George and the Spanish and Portuguese Prime Ministers. We were going to give Mr Hussein a Final Ultimatum and do A Show Of Unity so everyone could see just how United the International Community was behind the Threat of a War.

The Azores are famous because of a poem by Tennyson. This is the first line of that poem:

At Flores in the Azores Sir Richard Grenville lay

It is a poem about an English defeat at sea and the loss of a heroic captain.

17 March 2003
A Busy Day

We withdrew the Second Resolution from the table of The Security Council of The UN.

George delivered a speech giving Mr Hussein forty-eight hours to leave Iraq. And he told all foreign nationals to leave Iraq. Including the Weapons Inspectors.

I Thought About Resigning if the Vote went against me.

I sat down to write the Most Important Speech Of My Political Career.

And it wasn't just my future that depended on it but also the future of The Government and the future of The Country and the Future of The World.

That's how important it was and that's how important The Vote would be.

But the Good Thing was that I Knew How To Win Votes.

18 March 2003
Isn't Democracy Great!

The way we went about Winning Votes is the way that we always went about Winning Votes: we treated the whole thing like An Election.

And we always won Elections.

And just like in an Election What You Focus On Is Very Important. That's why I took so much time making sure that I was writing the Best Speech Ever. But just like in an Election what's more Important than What You Focus On is Who You Focus On.

There's no point Focusing On those who are going

to Vote For You. And there's no point Focusing On those who are going to Vote Against You. The only people that it Makes Sense to Focus On are the ones who Aren't Sure Yet. The ones who Are In Two Minds. The ones who Could Go Either Way.

And this is where, just like in an Election, you need to Know The People.

And we worked out a strategy to target each one.

Some could be Persuaded by talking about The Integrity Of The UN. Some could be Persuaded by talking about Mr Hussein and his Appalling Human Rights Record. Some could be Persuaded by talking about the Sneaky French. Some could be Persuaded by talking about How It Would Look If We Brought The Troops Back Now. And some could be Persuaded by talking about how 'Disappointed' I Would Be if they voted against Me.

And all the time we made sure The Big Guns of The Party kept Pounding Away. And that way, when I got up to speak in The House Of Commons, to give The Most Important Speech Of My Life, the groundwork had been done. And the Troops had been through Shock and Awe. And there were Great Big Holes In the Defences.

And the thing is, I'm Good At Making Speeches. I'm Very Good.

So They Voted For Me. They Would Have Been MAD not to.

And so I Won The Vote. And not only did I Win The Vote In The House, I also Won A Sizable Majority In The Parliamentary Labour Party. And I Won The Vote because I Was Ruthless and because I Seized The Moment which are all things you have to do when you want to Win An Election.

But I also Won The Vote because I did something Very Clever. The something Very Clever I did was I went beyond what you do at an Election. In an Election you look at your opponent's Strength and turn it into a Weakness but what I did was look at my Weakness and turn it into a Strength.

And my Weakness was that This Vote Might Be The End Of My Political Career.

And my Strength was that This Vote Might Be The End Of My Political Career.

And I made sure that everybody knew this. It was The Nuclear Option and I had my Finger On The Button.

And that's How I Won The Vote. So maybe the vote turned out to be about Regime Change after all.

The next day I put up a sign in The Den. It said:

PEACE IS OUR PROFESSION

And the day after that The War Started.
And the rest is history.

THE END

What Alastair Thought About It All

When I finished My Story I showed it to Alastair and asked him what he thought about it all. And this is what he said:

'Are you sure you want to say all this?'

And I said, 'Yes.'

And he said, 'I'm not convinced that you come out of it so well.'

And I said, 'Well, I think it just shows that I Was Right All Along About Everything and how I Had No Choice.'

And he said, 'OK, Tone, you're The Boss.'

And I said, 'Yes I am. And I Always Have Been. And I'm ready to Meet My Maker over the decisions I've taken.'

And Alastair said, 'Your Maker. That would be ... God?'

And I said, 'Well, who else could it be?'

But Alastair never answered me.

Outroduction

A lot of this book is made-up nonsense.
Unfortunately quite a lot of what it is based on isn't.

Bibliography

The stuff I didn't make up came from these books. I recommend all of them.

The Unfinished Revolution by Philip Gould (Little, Brown and Company 1998)

Blair's Wars by John Kampfner (The Free Press 2003)

Regime Unchanged. Why The War On Iraq Changed Nothing by Milan Rai (Pluto Press 2003)

The War We Could Not Stop. The Real Story Of The Battle For Iraq edited by Randeep Ramesh (Faber and Faber 2003)

Tony Blair. Prime Minister by John Rentoul (Little, Brown and Company 2001)

Tony Blair. In His Own Words edited by Paul Richards (Politico's Publishing 2004)

Hug Them Close. Blair, Clinton, Bush and the Special Relationship by Peter Riddell (Politico's Publishing 2003)

War On Iraq. What Team Bush Doesn't Want You To Know by Scott Ritter (Profile Books 2002)

Blair by Anthony Seldon (The Free Press 2004)

Journey's End by R. C. Sherriff (Penguin Books 1983; first published 1929)

The Iraq War Reader. History, Documents, Opinions edited by Micah L. Sifry and Christopher Cerf (Touchstone Books 2003)

Striking Terror. America's New War edited by Robert B. Silvers and Barbara Epstein (*New York Review Of Books* 2002)

The Wars Against Saddam. Taking The Hard Road To Baghdad by John Simpson (Macmillan 2003)

30 Days. A Month At The Heart Of Blair's War by Peter Stothard (HarperCollins 2003)

House Of Bush, House Of Saud by Craig Unger (Gibson Square Books 2004)

Julius Caesar York Notes For GCSE by Martin Walker (York Press 1998)

Plan Of Attack by Bob Woodward (Simon & Schuster 2004)

Who's Who

Me	Anthony Algernon St Michael (Tony) Blair, the Prime Minister
Alastair	Alastair Campbell, my Director of Communications
Anji	Anji Hunter, my friend, confidante and special assistant
Arsène Wenger	Manager of The Mighty Arsenal F.C.
Aussie Pete	Peter Thompson, my university days mentor
Bill	Bill Clinton, US President before George W. Bush
Mr Bin Laden	Osama Bin Laden, al-Qaeda leader
Mr Blix	Hans Blix, Chief UN Weapons Inspector
Carole	Carole Caplin, Cherry's lifestyle guru
Charlie	Charlie Falconer, longtime friend; now Lord Chancellor
Cherry	Cherie Blair, my wife
Clare	Clare Short, former International Development Secretary
Co-Lin	Colin Powell, US Secretary of State

Condoleezza	Condoleezza Rice, George W. Bush's National Security Adviser
David With The Dog	David Blunkett, the Home Secretary
Derek	Derek Hatton, 1980s Militant leader of Liverpool Council
Derry	Derry Irvine, my first boss when I became a lawyer; later Lord Chancellor
Dick	Dick Cheney, George Bush's Vice President
Don	Donald Rumsfeld, George W. Bush's Secretary of Defense
Mr Ecclestone	Bernie Ecclestone, Formula 1 Motor Racing supremo
Estelle	Estelle Morris, currently Minister for the Arts; formerly Education Secretary
Geoff	Geoff Hoon, the Defence Secretary
George	George W. Bush, the President of the United States
Gerhardt	Gerhardt Schroeder, the Chancellor of the Germans
God	God
Gordon	Gordon Brown, the Chancellor of the Exchequer
Mr Hussein	Saddam Hussein, the President of Iraq

Jack	Jack Straw, the Foreign Secretary
Jacques	Jacques Chirac, the President of France
Jonathan	Jonathan Powell, my Chief of Staff/Principal Private Secretary
Jo Moore	a handy scapegoat
Ken	Ken Livingstone, leader of the GLC before it was abolished
Kylie	Kylie Minogue, popular Australian chanteuse
Mo	Mo Mowlam, former Northern Ireland Secretary
Monica With The Stains	Monica Lewinsky, Bill Clinton's paramour
Peter M/Peter	Peter Mandelson
Philip With The Glasses	Philip Gould, my advertising and market research guru
Robin	Robin Cook, Leader of The House of Commons until he resigned over the War with Iraq
Roy With The Funny Rs	Roy Jenkins, ex Labour Party and founder of SDP
Mr Scarlett	John Scarlett, Head of the Joint Intelligence Committee
Vladimir	Vladimir Putin, the President of Russia

Who's Not Who

Mr Ahmed al-Baz

A Jordanian taxi driver killed on the road from Baghdad to Amman. The first confirmed casualty of the War. Died during a US missile attack aimed at assassinating Saddam Hussein. Mr al-Baz had stopped at a shop to phone his wife. There was no military site in the area; only a police station about a kilometre away.